GLIMPSES OF GLORY

GLIMPSES OF GLORY
Daily Reflections on the Bible

CAROL M. BECHTEL

Westminster John Knox Press
Louisville, Kentucky

Book design by Jennifer K. Cox
Cover design by Kevin Darst

First edition
Published by Westminster John Knox Press
Louisville, Kentucky

This book is printed on acid-free paper that meets the
American National Standards Institute Z39.48 standard. ♾

PRINTED IN THE UNITED STATES OF AMERICA
98 99 00 01 02 03 04 05 06 07 — 10 9 8 7 6 5 4 3 2 1

Library of Congress Cataloging-in-Publication Data

Bechtel, Carol, date.
Glimpses of glory : daily reflections on the Bible /
Carol Bechtel. — 1st ed.
      p.   cm.
  Includes bibliographical references.
  ISBN 0-664-25743-7 (alk. paper)
  1. Bible.—Meditations.   2. Spiritual life—Christianity.
3. Devotional calendars.   I. Title.
BS491.2.R48   1998
242′.5—dc21   97-41414

To my parents, Rhea and Glenn Bechtel,
who taught me to look for glimpses of glory.

CONTENTS

BIBLE PORTRAITS

PREFACE

Sometimes all it takes is a glimpse to keep us going. A navigator catches sight of the north star, and corrects the ship's course. We look into the eyes of someone who understands us, and we can face what is ahead with renewed courage.

Glimpses of Glory seeks to give us such glimpses into the Bible. Sometimes what we see will startle; sometimes it will console. Sometimes it will delight us with its humanity; other times it will drive us to our knees with its divinity. But always the glimpse will invite us into a more intimate relationship with the Bible and the God who is revealed to us in it.

Each meditation is based on a short scripture passage which should be read along with the study. (The New Revised Standard Version is a helpful and reliable translation, and is used for all quotes in the studies unless otherwise indicated.) Questions for discussion and/or reflection follow, making this a book that is easily adaptable for either individual or group use.

Some of the studies are attuned to a particular season of the church year. (This reflects the fact that they were originally written as monthly Bible study columns for the magazine *Presbyterians Today* and its predecessor

Preface

Presbyterian Survey.) Groups who use them on a monthly basis may want to take note of this and use them accordingly. The meditations are by no means limited to these special seasons, however, and may be read at any time and in any order. As the subtitle of this book indicates, they are certainly appropriate guides for daily meditation.

The book is divided into three sections of ten studies each. The first section, "Stories of God's Surprises," explores the ways in which God delights in the unexpected. Sometimes the surprise is on the biblical characters, and other times it is on us! Either way, these stories underscore the fact that God—while utterly faithful—is also utterly unpredictable.

The second set of studies deals with "Neglected Texts." These overlooked or misunderstood passages are often avoided out of confusion or discomfort, or they may simply have slipped into the shadows of more familiar verses. All of them, however, have much to offer those who dare to seek them out and dust them off.

The third section, "Bible Portraits," looks at biblical saints and sinners, seeking to recognize the ways in which their stories intersect with our own. These studies make a conscious attempt to get beyond the caricatures that often pass for portraits of these biblical characters. By portraying them in as full and faithful a way as possible, we hope that their lives and witnesses may be restored to contemporary Christians in fresh ways.

Preface

One final word: Although these studies were originally published in a Presbyterian magazine, they are by no means directed solely to Presbyterians. These glimpses are offered in the spirit of Isaiah 40:5, where we are assured that "the glory of the LORD shall be revealed, and all people shall see it together."

STORIES OF
GOD'S SURPRISES

TASTE AND SEE
John 4:1–42

he Samaritan woman got up that morning and donned her shame the same as any other morning. Little did she know she was dressing for the man of her dreams. She would have laughed at that prospect, though it would have been a hard, bitter laugh. She'd had five husbands already, after all, and the man snoring in her bed this morning hadn't even bothered to marry her. She needed another man like she needed a hole in her water jar. Besides, what respectable man would have her?

The morning was well along when she hoisted the jar onto her shoulder and set out for the well outside of town. It was hot—too late in the morning, really, for this sort of lifting and carrying. But she preferred to avoid the stares and whispers of the other women, so she had long ago stopped making the trip during the cool of the day.

The irony of her destination was not lost on her.[1] Jacob's well, they called it. It recalled the scene of a great historical romance. Father Jacob had won the heart of Mother Rachel at a well much like this one. The story was a favorite around the local campfires. Even the children knew Genesis 29 by heart: how Jacob, on the lam from his brother Esau, had wandered to the well, exhausted from his flight. And how, at the sight of his beautiful cousin Rachel, he had gotten a superhuman burst of energy and rolled the stone from the mouth of the well. She had run right home to tell her father. He must have been impressed, too, since he'd invited Jacob home for a month. It was the beginning of a beautiful, if complicated, relationship.

But that was another story, a very different story than any *she* could ever dream of. Best not even to think about it. Just lift and carry, lift and carry, day after day until she dropped.

She was startled out of her cynicism when the lone man at the well asked her for a drink. There were two good reasons to expect the silent treatment, as he was both Jewish and male. What was he up to, she wondered, striking up a conversation with her, a Samaritan woman? And why was he rambling on about "living water"? He had obviously been out in the sun too long.

"Are you greater than our ancestor Jacob, who gave us this well?" she had asked with a sarcastic edge to her voice.

If she had expected him to take offense, she was surprised. He hadn't. He had just kept on about the living water, explaining it patiently, as if to a beloved child.

Well, he might be crazy, but he knew how to pitch a product. What a luxury not to have to run the gauntlet of those accusing stares every day! Cynicism gave way to wistfulness as she said, "Sir, give me this water, so that I may never be thirsty or have to keep coming here to draw water."

The rest of the story, of course, is a favorite around the local campfires. How Jesus had told her to call her husband, knowing full well that she had none (or perhaps too many!). That had unnerved her, but he had seemed pleased when she owned up to the truth. What was the use of hiding something, after all, from someone who could obviously see right into her soul? The truth had dawned on her gradually: this was no ordinary man. This was the Messiah.

She had run back to the village just like Mother Rachel, no longer ashamed, but honored to be the bearer of such astonishing news. The villagers must have sensed the difference in her, because they had followed her back to the well without a word.

They had arrived just in time to hear Jesus refusing to eat the food that the disciples were trying hard to force upon him. Jesus, it seems, was saving himself for another feast. Just as Father Jacob had come back to celebrate with Rachel's family, so Jesus had returned to the village for a two-day celebration with the Samaritans. It had taken the disciples a while to enter into the festivities, but they had warmed up to it eventually.

Not everyone in the village had bought into Jesus' offer of living water. There were some who had kept their teeth clenched and their eyes and ears tightly shut. But many others had believed. As for the Samaritan woman, she never tired of pleading with people—no matter how tainted their past—to "taste and see that the LORD is good" (Ps. 34:8).

FOR REFLECTION:

1. Do you have anything in your life that you are trying to hide from God?

2. If you were to have a conversation with Jesus similar to the one the Samaritan woman had, how might it go? What changes might take place in your life as a result?

THE BRIGHT SIDE
OF THE FALL

Genesis 3

t first glance the only surprising thing about "the fall" is that it takes until the third chapter of Genesis to get around to it. Two whole chapters of holy writ pass before we get to the story of how humanity oversteps God's gracious limits and decides to go it alone.

Yet closer scrutiny reveals several other surprises, albeit more subtle ones. Eve, for instance, though traditionally depicted as the temptress (Milton describes Adam as being "fondly overcome by female charm"), could better be characterized as an unwitting participant in the first theological debate.[2] The crafty (though not necessarily evil) serpent throws her off balance with his opening argument. "Did God say," he asks in verse 1, "'You shall not eat from *any* tree in the garden'?" This, of course, overstates God's original instructions in 2:16–17. Eve jumps to God's defense and, for good measure, overstates her interpretation of God's injunction as well. They are only prohibited from one tree, she tells him, and in fact (this is where she exaggerates), it is death even to touch it (3:3). Having thus successfully upset Eve's theological equilibrium, the serpent strikes while Eve is off balance. "You won't die," he reassures her in verse 4; the real issue is the knowledge of good and evil—a godly quality if ever there was one. Eve, reasoning perhaps that a mind is a terrible thing to waste, "falls" for this appealing argument and sinks her teeth into the fateful fruit. Her husband, who has evidently been standing meekly by all the while (3:6), eats right along with her.

The scene that ensues is all too familiar and can hardly qualify as a surprise to anyone remotely acquainted with the current condition of human nature. When confronted by God (vv. 8–13), Adam and Eve strive valiantly to pass the buck. Yet God is not fooled by their finger-pointing. Verses 14–19 detail the terrible consequences of their disobedience. We should not miss the fact, however, that it is only the serpent who is *cursed* for his actions (vv. 14–15). The human couple, on the other hand, is not cursed, but consigned to struggle incessantly with a natural world that will no longer cooperate. Work, which was originally part of God's good creation (see 2:15), now becomes toil. Childbearing, which was initially part of God's joyous command of fruitfulness (see 1:28), now becomes labor. It is not a blissful existence, but neither is it devoid of all fulfillment and grace.

The biggest surprise in this story, however, lies in its smallest detail. It is a detail often overlooked in the drama of the expulsion from the garden, but it is of immense importance for those of us who make our homes here on the eastern edge of Eden.

Verse 21 tells us that God clothes Adam and Eve with garments made of animal skins. It seems a small thing, yet it prepares the pair for their entry into their new and often hostile environment. And it prepares us for the fact that God's love for us supersedes our sinfulness. In fact, it hints at the possibility that there is a strange and wonderful sequel to this archetypal story.

Edwin Muir, the twentieth-century Scottish poet, captures this surprising angle in his poem entitled, "One Foot in Eden." Crassly put, he suggests that there is a "bright side" to the fall. "Famished field and blackened tree," he reminds us, "bear flowers in Eden never known. . . ."

> Blossoms of grief and charity
> Bloom in these darkened fields alone.
> What had Eden ever to say
> Of hope and faith and pity and love . . .
> Strange blessings never in Paradise
> Fall from these beclouded skies.[3]

Strange blessings, indeed. While one can hardly be happy about the fall, one can hardly be sorry about the resurrection. In fact, the path to Bethlehem, Golgotha, and the empty tomb is strewn with what Muir terms "blossoms of grief and charity." His poetry reminds us that the seeds of "hope and faith and pity and love" were all planted that day at the edge of the garden. It is a mystery—a paradox—a supreme surprise. While we cannot understand it, we can surely celebrate it. It is, after all, the bright side of the fall.

FOR REFLECTION:

1. What surprises did you encounter in the retelling of this familiar story?

2. Does this ancient story explain anything about your own life experience? If so, what?

3. Do you agree that there might be a "bright side" to the fall?

WHEN GOD
TESTS OUR METAL
Genesis 22

"his is a test. This is only a test. In the event of an actual emergency. . . ." The opening verse of Genesis 22 sounds a lot like that familiar announcement from the Emergency Broadcast System. "After these things," it says, "God tested Abraham. . . ." The difference is that we, the readers, know that it is "only" a test, but from Abraham's perspective the emergency is very real. God has asked him to sacrifice his son, the child of the promise (Gen. 12:1–3; 15:1–6). Thus, the personal ramifications of the command are as devastating as the theological ones. Yet, as nonsensical as that order must have seemed, Abraham has no indication whatsoever that it is a drill.

How does it help to know that Abraham's ordeal was, in fact, a test? At first glance, it doesn't. There are many levels at which modern readers may be horrified by this ancient story. Attuned as we are to issues of child abuse, we worry quite rightly about the trauma this so-called test would have inflicted on the innocent Isaac. And what about Sarah? She certainly stood to lose much in this attempt to ascertain her husband Abraham's faithfulness.

(This angle on the story has led one feminist interpreter to label the story "The Sacrifice of Sarah.") Last but not least, the hapless Abraham elicits our sympathies, caught as he is in the excruciating conflict between mutually exclusive promise and command.

Surely, a God who could stage such an exam is inconsiderate at best and capricious at worst. If this is one of God's "surprises," then it seems a rather sinister one!

Perhaps part of our problem with this story is in our narrow, and largely negative, understanding of the word "test." We tend to associate it with nervous cramming, sweaty palms, and unrealistic time limits ("Stop. Put your pencils down."). We sometimes forget that a test can be an opportunity for growth, for creativity, and for strengthening the knowledge we already have.

Psalm 26:2 suggests that the biblical use of the idea of a "test" has just such creative connotations. In that verse the psalmist asks to be tested, and to be tried and proven. These other two words are intriguing because of their close association (in Hebrew) with the process by which metals are refined. This procedure involves heating the metal to extremely high temperatures in order to remove all impurities. The result is a product that is significantly finer, purer, and stronger. What would happen if we were to read Genesis 22 again within this "refined" framework?

First, we might notice that in spite of the fact that the story is brutally bare in terms of the characters' emotional turmoil, there are several suggestive details that testify to the pain in this process of refinement. Although Abraham loves his son Isaac (v. 2), he does not hesitate, but rises "early in the morning" to embark on that fateful journey toward the land of Moriah. Throughout the story he takes pains to shield Isaac from the knowledge of the nature of their trip. For example, he tells the servants in verse 5, "we will worship, and then we will come back to you," and his diplomatic response to Isaac's query about the whereabouts of the sacrificial lamb in verses 7–8 is "God himself will provide the lamb for a burnt offering, my son." Finally, there is the care he shows as he distributes the load for the last leg of their journey. Isaac, ironically, must carry the wood for his own immolation, but Abraham carries the dangerous elements of fire and knife.

All of these examples reveal a man whose "metal" is being severely tested. It is a painful, even excruciating, process. Yet he endures it with courage, compassion, and considerable creativity—all without knowing that he is, indeed, being tested.

As Christians, we live out our lives caught in the painful paradox of realities that do not conform to the full realization of God's promises. Children are killed by violent storms even as they rehearse their hallelujahs. We confess the resurrection of the dead at the graves of our loved ones. Our churches divide in rancor even as we unite to worship the Prince of Peace.

As readers of Genesis 22, however, we are given a significant advantage over Father Abraham. First, we know how the story begins. It is identified from the outset as a "test," and, as we have seen, a test can be a process by which our faith is refined. Second, and even more important, we know how the story ends. God does indeed provide the Lamb, both for Isaac and the world. It is the knowledge of that "surprise ending" that gives us courage to make our own way toward the land of Moriah. It is that knowledge that enables us to bear the pain when God "tests our metal."

FOR REFLECTION:

1. Has God ever called you to do something that seemed inconsistent with God's own previous promises? How did you handle it? How do you feel about the experience now?

2. How do you feel about God in this story? About Abraham? About Isaac? About Sarah?

A THEOLOGICAL
REALITY CHECK
Deuteronomy 7:6–11

S. Lewis once observed that reality is generally something you'd never expect.[4] In a world filled with "wonder-ful" realities like basset hounds, jellyfish, and hummingbirds, who could argue with that observation? Which of us, even in our wildest imagination, could have predicted that God would pencil such impractical creatures onto creation's calendar? If we have eyes to see, they are among the many reminders of the utterly unpredictable nature of the reality in which we live and move and have our being.

Perhaps we do not need to look any further than the end of our own noses, however, for a prime example of Lewis's unexpected reality. Humanity has to be one of God's most fanciful creative ventures. Never mind that we are "fearfully and wonderfully made" (Ps. 139:14). The biggest surprise arises from the ways in which God has chosen to relate to us over the centuries. The Bible chronicles this old, old story from the standpoint of faith, and it portrays our God as a God who is singularly unimpressed by our most magnificent achievements. In fact, if salvation history is any indication, it would appear that God regularly sidesteps our expectations and exercises a preferential option for the underdog.

We can see this working its way out in any number of biblical passages, but perhaps nowhere so overtly as in Deuteronomy 7:6–11. Before we talk about its content, however, let's take a moment to review this passage's context.

The people of God are perched on the brink of the promised land. It is a time of great expectations and exhilarating anticipation. If we as readers have been perseverent enough to read the Pentateuch like a novel, we will have realized that all of the plot's momentum has our heroes and heroines rushing headlong toward the promised land. It is strange, under such literary circumstances, that the plot grinds so suddenly to a halt at the eastern edge of the River Jordan (Deut. 1:1–5). We, along with the excited Israelites, are brought up short and forced to listen to the lengthy sermon that we now call the book of Deuteronomy. How ironic it is that this company of former slaves should so quickly become a captive audience.

The content of this sermon is infused with irony as well. Just as they are on the verge of receiving their inheritance, the children of Israel are reminded that they are not, in fact, such "hot stuff." Deuteronomy 7:6–11 serves as an important theological reality check. It begins with a lavish announcement of the people's election as God's own holy and treasured possession (v. 6), but then follows with an abrupt application of cold water. Just so they (and we) don't get the wrong idea, God quickly reminds them that their favored status has nothing to do with their own merits. "It was not because you were more numerous than any other people that the Lord set his heart on you and chose you," God informs them in verse 7, for, in fact, "you were the fewest of all peoples."

Well, if not numbers, then what?

Love, as they say, is the answer (v. 8). Love and a promise made long ago to the people's ancestors. So much for smugness. Election is a supreme, though not altogether flattering, surprise, and one which every baptized Christian experiences at the baptismal font. We are loved, pure and simple, not because of our accomplishments or our beauty, our strength or our intelligence, but just *because*. And who can explain the "why" of this ancient yet ever-new love story? God's ways are not necessarily our ways, nor God's thoughts our thoughts (Isa. 55:8). The reality of redemption is infused, not just with irony, but with grace. And it is a reality that far, far exceeds our wildest expectations.

FOR REFLECTION:

1. What is the most extravagant example of God's playful creativity in nature? What does the creature reveal about the Creator?

2. Why should Christians obey God's commandments? If merit is not the motive, then what is?

DIAGNOSIS: DISASTER
Jeremiah 7:1–15

ou have just been wheeled into the emergency room with a severed artery. As you slip from consciousness, your last impression is of the attending physician glancing nonchalantly over the top of your chart and dismissing your wound as "superficial."

This scene is preposterous. No modern emergency room would be guilty of such gross negligence. But it is just this sort of misdiagnosis that was made by the priests and prophets of Jeremiah's day. The political and religious situation was extremely grave. Babylon, like the grim reaper, was swinging its scythe ever closer to Jerusalem. The prophet Jeremiah, however, seemed to be the only one who was concerned. As Israel's lifeblood spurted away, he knew that the only appropriate course of action was repentance. But the nation's leaders did not seem to see any cause for alarm. They kept right on going through the motions of organized religion, downplaying the Babylonian threat, and counseling, "Peace, peace," when, as Jeremiah pointed out, there was no peace (6:14).

Jeremiah characterized the official predictions of peace in medical terms. He said the leaders had "treated the wound of my people carelessly" (6:14). Like the emergency room physician of our opening illustration, they had diagnosed a critical injury as a mere scratch. A doctor who pronounces, "Health, health," when there is no health is not doing the patient any favors.

Jeremiah delivered God's diagnosis in the form of a sermon that is preserved in the Bible twice—from Jeremiah's point of view (Jer. 7) and from the perspective of his secretary, Baruch (Jer. 26). It is from Baruch's account that we learn about the people's reaction. The reviews, it seems, were as unfavorable as they were immediate. After delivering the sermon Jeremiah was summarily arrested and accused of both blasphemy and treason.

What had Jeremiah said to get people so upset? He had simply observed that the temple was no guarantee of God's favor. The temple had been the grounds for the leadership's bravado in the face of the Babylonian foes. God would not dare to destroy the temple, they reasoned. So they rubbed it like a rabbit's foot every time the Babylonian scythe swung by.

In words suffused with sarcasm, Jeremiah quoted his opponents: "This is the temple of the Lord, the temple of the Lord, the temple of the Lord" (7:4). In the mouth of the prophet their pious platitudes were transformed into a child's mocking rhyme. The temple was no talisman against disaster, he warned. In fact, their attitude toward it was deceptive, dangerous, and deadly.

After outlining a more appropriate brand of piety in verses 5–10 (a piety that did not confuse form with substance!), Jeremiah reminded them that Shiloh had also been the site of a favored sanctuary. Yet Shiloh lay in ruins. It was a sobering precedent, for it demonstrated that God was not above burning down a house of worship if it would effectively cauterize worship's gaping wound.

Baruch's description of this sermon's aftermath suggests that Jeremiah definitely had struck a nerve. And the comeuppance he gave to the religious community of his day issues a warning to us as well. Not all of God's surprises are pleasant ones. No individuals or institutions can be confident that they have God in their pockets. For when the substance of our piety disappears, then the form is dispensable as well.

Are we ever guilty of diagnosing "health, health" when there is no health? How much better it is to face our condition honestly and to approach God with humility. How much better simply to say what Jeremiah taught us: "Heal me, O Lord, and I shall be healed; save me, and I shall be saved; for you are my praise" (17:14).

I MUST BE DREAMING
Psalm 126

asual observers would have considered the young couple obvious candidates for divorce. Their arguments were often embarrassingly public. Even in their less tumultuous moments their relationship seemed to lack a certain spark.

Jane Marple, however, is not just a casual observer. As the beloved octogenarian detective in many of Agatha Christie's mystery novels, Miss Marple has a way of seeing beyond the obvious. When she trains her detective's eye on the fictional couple in question, she sees possibilities that have eluded everyone else. With a tilt of her head and a wry, wrinkled smile, she suggests that they are simply slow starters. She then predicts that they will indeed fall in love, probably sometime after the birth of their third child.

We cannot all be as clairvoyant as Miss Marple, nor as fortunate as that young couple. Yet Miss Marple's intuitive prediction reminds us of something important, namely, that probability does not preclude possibility. Or as Yogi Berra once put it, "It ain't over 'til it's over."

Nowhere is this truism more true than in the Bible. In

fact, when God gets involved, we should probably give up talking about probabilities altogether. Over and over again, the Bible bears witness to a God who makes a habit of surprise endings, especially those that involve bringing life out of death.

Psalm 126 is one of these stories of God's surprises. "When the Lord restored the fortunes of Zion," it begins, "we were like those who dream." These words probably recall the surprise ending to the Babylonian exile, when Judah's captives were brought home and the city of Jerusalem (or Zion) was given a new lease on life. The experience was so unexpected and so unprecedented that it really qualifies as more of a resurrection than a restoration. The psalm thus begins with this sense of "pinch me, I must be dreaming." Through the psalmist's eyes we see the awestruck faces of the erstwhile exiles, their mouths "filled with laughter," their tongues "with shouts of joy" (v. 2).

The psalmist's celebration is not purely personal, however. Part of the intensity of that dream-like experience arises from the knowledge that God's reputation has been vindicated before the nations. "What will the neighbors say?" is a much more ancient question than most of us realize. Indeed, Moses used it as an argument to dissuade God from destroying the newborn Hebrew nation after the golden calf episode at Sinai (Ex. 32:12). The exile made it look like God had either given up caring about what the neighboring nations thought or, worse, was powerless to save the covenant people. With the restoration, however, rumors such as these could finally be laid to rest.

Stories of God's Surprises

In Psalm 126:2 even the nations are forced to admit that "the Lord has done great things for them."

Praise turns abruptly to petition in verse 4. "Restore our fortunes," the psalmist pleads. At this point we realize that the recollections of divine rescue in verses 1–3 have not been random. The memories of miraculous restoration in those verses serve both to praise and to pressure the Almighty. The gist of the psalmist's argument is "OK, God. You came through for them; now what about us?"

What was the psalmist's situation? We have no way of knowing. While that lack of specificity is a source of frustration to biblical scholars, it is actually a source of blessing for believers. Released from the particulars of one ancient author's problems, the psalm is set free to serve as a prayer for all believers who find themselves in apparently hopeless situations. Perhaps like Miss Marple's young couple, it is our marriage that seems to be running as dry as a parched riverbed. The psalm reminds us—and God—that even the dry watercourses of the wilderness can turn into raging torrents with the onset of the rainy season (v. 4). Perhaps we have shed countless tears over the loss of a loved one, a career, or a dream. Psalm 126 reminds us that "those who sow in tears" may, in God's surprising harvest, "reap with shouts of joy" (vv. 5–6).

Such surprise endings may be difficult for us to imagine as we wallow in an apparently hopeless present. We must remember, however, that God "is able to accomplish abundantly far more than all we can ask or imagine" (Eph. 3:20). Probabilities aside, there may yet be a day when people look at us and say, "The Lord has done great things for them." There may yet be a day when we look at each other in wonder and say, "Pinch me, I must be dreaming."

FOR REFLECTION:

1. Have you ever had an experience like that of the exiles? What did it feel like?

2. What would it mean to really believe that "with God all things are possible"?

3. Does God ever answer our prayers in unexpected ways?

THIS LITTLE BABE

Luke 2:1–20

t the heart of our faith lies a surprising paradox: power made perfect in weakness (2 Cor. 12:9). The story of Jesus' birth plays that paradox for all it's worth, or at least it does if we can get past the domesticated depictions of the nativity so familiar from Christmas cards and Holly Hobby children's books. Far truer to the shocking subtext of Luke 2 is Frederick Buechner's description of what really happened out there in the barn that first Christmas Eve. Incarnation, Buechner reminds us, "is not tame," but nothing less than "Ultimate Mystery born with a skull you could crush one-handed."[5] To say with the gospel of John that "the Word became flesh and dwelt among us" is a radical claim, and one that caught and continues to catch this waiting world completely off guard.

Power made perfect in weakness—who could have predicted it? Perhaps the Old Testament prophets were the only ones with any inkling. Scattered throughout the book of Isaiah, for example, are passages that seem to anticipate this inexplicable habit of God's heart. Isaiah 9 refers to a child born "for us" with the unlikely names:

Glimpses of Glory

Wonderful Counselor, Mighty God, Everlasting Father, Prince of Peace. Isaiah 53 drops hints about a Suffering Servant who "had no form or majesty that we should look at him," a man "despised and rejected . . . as one from whom others hide their faces." Yet this same social pariah is the one who was wounded for our transgressions, "by whose bruises we are healed." Whether one views these passages as pure prediction or as reflective of some now-forgotten situation in an earlier century, they give us a glimpse of God's proclivity for this particular paradox.

In a poem entitled "This Little Babe," a sixteenth-century priest named Robert Southwell plays on this paradox as well. (Some may be familiar with this poem from its musical setting in Benjamin Britten's *A Ceremony of Carols*.) Southwell writes,

> This little Babe so few days old,
> Is come to rifle Satan's fold,
> All hell doth at his presence quake,
> Though he himself for cold do shake;
> For in this weak unarmed wise
> The gates of hell he will surprise.
>
> With tears he fights and wins the field,
> His naked breast stands for a shield,
> his battering shot are babish cries,
> His arrows looks of weeping eyes,
> His martial ensigns Cold and Need,
> And feeble Flesh his warrior's steed.
>
> His camp is pitched in a stall,
> His bulwark but a broken wall;
> The crib his trench, haystalks his stakes;
> Of shepherds he his muster makes;

Stories of God's Surprises

> And thus, as sure his foe to wound,
> The angels' trumps alarum sound.[6]

The prevailing metaphor in this poem is in itself paradoxical: military imagery is used to describe the Prince of Peace. Yet the paradox runs even deeper. The imagery of this poem depicts a pitched battle waged in gruesome medieval style. There are shields, arrows, war horses, bulwarks, trenches, and stakes. Yet who is manning this mighty war machine but a baby. A very special baby, but nonetheless, a baby. To quote Buechner again, it is none other than the one "Omnipotent Baby."

The Christmas story is a wonderful, mind-boggling paradox that should never cease to surprise us. Who would have thought it? Who could have guessed? But then, it is part of a larger story well-stocked with surprises from start to finish. Consider the source. Given the surprising habit of God's heart, perhaps we should not be so astonished after all to meet a Savior

> who, though he was in the form of God, did not count equality with God a thing to be grasped, but emptied himself, being born in the likeness of humans. And being found in human form he humbled himself and became obedient unto death, even death on a cross (Phil. 2:6–8).

Perhaps we should *not* be surprised to peer into the manger and see "Ultimate Mystery born with a skull you could crush one-handed." Perhaps we should *not* be surprised to find the Lord of the Universe wrapped in swaddling cloths, nuzzling for his mother's breast. Perhaps we should *not* be surprised to find power made perfect in weakness.

29

FOR REFLECTION:

1. To what extent do your Christmas celebrations reflect the radical nature of the Word made flesh?

2. In what ways is Jesus' incarnation comforting? Frightening?

3. Does the paradox of "power made perfect in weakness" have any implications for the way Christians live their lives? If so, what are some of those implications?

HEARSAY CHRISTIANS
John 20:19–31

ven a casual fan of courtroom drama knows that hear-say is not admissible as evidence in a court of law. Whether we learned this at the feet of Atticus Finch, Perry Mason, or Robert Shapiro, we living-room lawyers will object with the best of them when anything less than firsthand testimony finds its way into the witness box.

Maybe that's the one reason modern men and women have so much trouble with that greatest of all God's surprises: the resurrection. We have it in our heads that "seeing is believing," and we did not, after all, witness it with our own eyes. No one did. Nor were we privy to any of the postresurrection appearances recorded in the gospels. So we are left with the accounts of the gospels themselves. Is there anything there capable of convincing a reasonable, rational citizen of the twentieth century that the resurrection was anything more than the wishful thinking of a bunch of disillusioned disciples? Can we admit their "testimony" without having to resort to mere hearsay?

The gospels claim to bear witness to what was handed on "by those who from the beginning were eyewitnesses and servants of the word" (Luke 1:2). Even if we allow for a certain amount of theological shaping in the different gospel accounts, this would seem to meet fairly high standards of evidence. Yet nowhere in any of the gospels do we encounter as credible a witness as Thomas. In him our twentieth-century skepticism meets its match.

The resurrection caught poor Thomas by surprise. John 20 tells the story of how he returned to the locked house where he and the other disciples had been hiding to find his friends fairly bursting with the news that they had seen their crucified Lord alive and well.

We cannot read Thomas's mind. Perhaps the detail of the locked doors led him to believe that his friends had seen some sort of phantom. Perhaps he knew how badly they all wanted to believe. Whatever the reason, his skeptical response has earned him the derogatory nickname that has dogged him ever since: Doubting Thomas. "Unless I see the mark of the nails in his hands," he insisted, "and put my finger in the mark of the nails and my hand in his side, I will not believe" (v. 25). For Thomas, not even seeing was believing; he wanted to touch too!

Thomas's demands were so incredible that one suspects he was being facetious when he made them. He didn't really expect Jesus to show up and say, "OK, here you are." Imagine his surprise!

Imagine ours as well. Here, tucked into the New Testament itself is a story that anticipates our skepticism point for point. Thomas's story bears witness to the fact that there were those present in the days of Christianity's infancy who were slow to believe in the resurrection. They were not about to be duped into believing what they wanted to believe so badly. For all of the bad press that "Doubting Thomas" has received over the centuries, it is that very tendency to doubt that makes him such a compelling apostle to us, the hearsay Christians. As witnesses go, he is the best. Yet even he concludes with a confession, "My Lord and my God!" (v. 28).

As a whole the gospel of John seems to have an extra measure of sensitivity for those of us who would come to the resurrection long after the fact. It is as if John had a special insight into the peculiar hazards that would confront the faith of hearsay Christians. "Blessed are those who have not seen and yet have come to believe," he records Jesus as saying at the end of this story about Thomas (v. 29). And earlier, when Jesus prays for his disciples in the garden, he prays, "I ask not only on behalf of these, but also on behalf of those who will believe in me through their word" (John 17:20). That's us—the hearsay Christians. We have not seen with our own eyes. Yet we can rely on the testimony of those who did. We believe through their word, and believing, we have life in Jesus' name (John 20:31).

LEOPARDS AND
THEIR SPOTS
Acts 9:1–22

ld habits die hard. You can't teach an old dog new tricks. Can the leopard change its spots?

Old proverbs die hard, too, as the three preceding examples illustrate. Most of us grew up hearing them. And unless human nature undergoes some radical modifications in the near future, most of our grandchildren will grow up hearing them. Their longevity reflects their reliability. They bear witness to something that is as basic to our nature as eating, breathing, and sleeping, namely, our tendency to resist change.

In the face of these reflections on the inflexibility of human nature, we are brought up short by this peculiar passage from Acts. It bears witness to some surprising departures from the proverbial in that it gives an account of at least two instances of overcoming the behavioral odds.

First, there is the story of Paul's conversion, a story so famous for its radical reversal that any equally dramatic change of heart is often described as a "Damascus Road" experience. Paul starts out for Damascus planning to take Christ's confessors captive. Instead, he ends up being taken captive himself, a captive of the Risen Christ.

Glimpses of Glory

The surprise in this story is definitely on Paul. Yet we should not overlook Ananias in our tally of drastic instances of behavior modification. Chances are that if Ananias had spent hours compiling his agenda for that day, he would never have penciled in "Visit Paul; do baptism." God's instructions to go and look for Saul (later called Paul) on the street called Straight (vv. 11–12) must have struck Ananias as the height of lunacy! All the Christians in Damascus must have been doing their utmost to *avoid* Saul, given his reputation as a self-appointed persecutor of Christians. Notice how vivid the characterization of his activities is in 9:1. Anyone who could be described as "breathing threats and murder against the disciples of the Lord," was not someone to be toyed with (see also Gal. 1:13).

Ananias is diplomatically doubtful in his response (vv. 13–14) and, as such, stands in a long line of biblical figures who have dared to respond to God's orders with "Yes, but. . . . " That he dared to differ at all with the Almighty is an index of how deeply shocked he must have been at the idea that Saul was to be the instrument by which God's name was to be brought "before Gentiles and kings and before the people of Israel" (v. 15).

Finally, however, Ananias surmounts his fears and goes to visit the street called Straight. When he arrives at the appointed house, he finds a Saul much changed. One has to wonder if, even at this point, Ananias did not fear a trap. What if it was all a setup? What if Saul was only putting on a charade designed to flush out unsuspecting Christians? If Ananias was worried, he did not let on. Instead, he laid healing hands on the man who had caused

36

hurting hands to be laid upon so many. The Church has never been the same since.

So what can we conclude from this story? Are Paul and Ananias exceptions to the rule of human inflexibility? Are they superhumans who can "change their spots" after all?

The point of this passage, it seems to me, is not that Paul and Ananias are so much more heroic than the rest of us. It is that God has the power to change us, sometimes even in spite of ourselves. This is the truth that can give us hope in the face of all of those depressing proverbs about the improbability of human change. If we were to go back, in light of this passage, to the proverb about that hypothetical leopard and ask, "Can the leopard change its spots?" the answer would have to be "No, the leopard can't—but *God* can." If there are spots in our lives that need changing, then we would do well to remember who created that leopard in the first place!

Glimpses of Glory

FOR REFLECTION:

1. Do your prayers take into consideration God's capacity to effect surprising changes?

2. Have you ever prayed for something for a long time without results? What does this say about God?

IF I SHOULD DIE . . .
I Corinthians 15:50–58

ave you ever walked in on the end of a heated argument? Reading only the last eight verses of Paul's "immortal" chapter on the resurrection is a little like that. You can feel the intensity and sense the passion, but you can only begin to guess at the rhetorical thrusts and parries that must have gone before. Paul can parry with the best of them. First Corinthians 15:1–49 represents one of the most tightly constructed arguments in all of scripture. In this passage, Paul fights for the faith of those Corinthian Christians who were wavering on the question of whether Christ really rose from the dead, and of whether we as his followers should live in expectation of the same.

Most of Paul's arguments seem to be directed at those who are advocating the immortality of the soul rather than the resurrection of the body. Most modern Christians have not thought much about the difference. We sing blithely through hymn texts like this one by Charles Wesley:

A charge to keep I have; A God to glorify,
A never-dying soul to save, And fit it for the sky.

Glimpses of Glory

Yet we fail to realize that we are singing something that is fundamentally unbiblical. Never-dying souls, after all, have no need of the resurrection. They are perfectly capable of flying off to heaven—or wherever—under their own speed.

I hope that the above comments are provocative enough to send you straight to your Bibles for a careful reading of 1 Corinthians 15 in its entirety. Beware, however, of getting too caught up in the argumentative fray. Notice that Paul does not end with arguments. Finally, in the last eight verses of the chapter he falls back on what he openly acknowledges as "mystery" (v. 51). Not even Paul would dare to explain what will happen to us in that moment when, in the twinkling of an eye, our mortal *bodies* put on immortality and Death itself will be "swallowed up in victory" (vv. 52–55).

Perhaps Paul knew that what the Corinthian Christians really wanted was comfort. The intensity of their arguments—and our own—are symptoms of our deepest fears. What will happen to us when we die? Will we ever see our loved ones again? Is death the end after all?

Emily Dickinson articulates some of these questions in her poem "I know that He exists."[7] The poem begins with almost playful images of death. She pictures it as a "fond Ambush," designed "to make Bliss earn her own surprise." Yet what if the surprise were to turn sour? What if the "play" should "prove piercing earnest" and "the glee glaze in Death's stiff stare?" "Would not the fun" then "look too expensive?" Dickinson asks. "Would not the just" then "have crawled too far"?

Dickinson's poem raises the chilling possibility of what

would happen if all of our worst fears were realized. These fears are as old as the Corinthians and as new as last night's bedtime prayers ("If I should die before I wake . . . "). They haunt us in hospital rooms, at gravesides, and even at children's birthday parties. They whisper their "what ifs" in our ear while the communion wine is still on our tongue. And they remind us that, where death is concerned, we are in no mood for surprises—especially unpleasant ones!

In the face of these fears there is only one remedy. Paul applies it with a gentle and knowing hand. In these last verses, Paul quietly reminds us that it is not *what* we know but *whom* we know. It is, after all, "*our* Lord Jesus Christ" who has removed the "sting" from death and "gives *us* the victory." What greater comfort could we ask for than that we belong—body and/or soul—to our faithful savior, Jesus Christ?

FOR REFLECTION:

1. Do you believe in the resurrection of the body or the immortality of the soul? What difference does it make?

2. Is one of these views more comforting to you than the other? If so, why?

3. How do Paul's words from Romans 14:8 ("... whether we live or whether we die, we are the Lord's.") factor into your reflections?

NEGLECTED
TEXTS

PICTURES OF PRAYER
Psalm 131

omplete the following sentence:

My prayers most closely resemble

A)   a grocery list.

B)   a subpoena.

C)   a love letter.

D)   a blank page.

There is no right answer to the above question, and the choices are hardly exhaustive. We might answer differently depending on the situation. Yet all of the answers nudge us out of the abstract and invite us to picture our prayer life in a startlingly graphic way. We can learn a great deal about our relationship with God through such an exercise. After all, a picture paints a thousand words!

Psalm 131 presents us with another powerful picture of the believer at prayer. "O LORD, my heart is not lifted up," its author asserts. "My eyes are not raised too high. I do not occupy myself with things too great and too marvelous for me" (v. 1). To illustrate this attitude, the psalmist then offers God—and us—a visual aid. "I have calmed and quieted my soul," the author writes, "like a weaned child with its mother" (v. 2a).

The power of this picture is often lost on modern readers. One of the reasons for this is that some Bible translations actually obscure the passage's main point. The Revised Standard Version, for instance, translates the key phrase as "like a child quieted at its mother's breast." While this presents a lovely picture, it is not the one the psalmist intends. The force of the psalmist's imagery resides in the use of a Hebrew word that means not just "child" but "weaned child."

This brings us to the second reason this passage is both overlooked and misunderstood. Many of us are not familiar enough with the process of breast-feeding to know that there is a dramatic difference in the behavior of a child that has been weaned and one that has not. In contrast to the child who is still nursing, a weaned child can enjoy closeness with its mother without always clamoring for the fulfillment of its wants. An awareness of this difference is critical for understanding what the psalmist is saying.

How often do we relate to God like a weaned child? Are we ever just content to enjoy God's intimate presence, or is prayer only an opportunity for us to clamor for what's coming to us? While it is true that the Bible encourages us to "let [our] requests be made known to God" (Phil. 4:6), this psalm reminds us that there is more to prayer than just the fulfillment of our wants and needs.

Prayer for the mature believer is meant to be a time of intimate communion and quiet trust.

This brings us to yet another reason for this psalm's being a "neglected text." The picture it paints is one of humble submission to God's will. This is an attitude that has never been popular or easily achieved in any age. Aren't there, however, some situations in which we must all come into our Lord's presence ready to say, "Not my will, but yours be done"? When we are in such a situation, this psalm may be just what we need to gather the courage to say those difficult words. Its graphic imagery reminds us that, like a weaned child with its mother, we can relax and trust ourselves to that intimate Presence to whom all our wants are known.

FOR REFLECTION:

1. To what extent does this psalm's picture of prayer describe your prayer life?

2. When do you find it most difficult to pray, "Not my will, but yours be done"?

JUST AN OLD-FASHIONED LOVE SONG
Song of Solomon 4:1–5:1

 as your teenager been reading the Bible a lot lately? Do you find this behavior suspiciously out of character? If so, it is possible that he or she may be sneaking a peek at the Song of Solomon. A brief glance at chapter 4 of this Old Testament book will suffice to explain this newfound fascination. This representative passage describes the various parts of a woman's body, starting with her eyes and moving tenderly downward. In language that is both provocative and poetic, the author lingers over his lover's most tantalizing features, until finally, the poem breaks off with an admonition to "be drunk with love" (5:1).

While our first instinct might be to ask, "Is this stuff really in the Bible?" our second is to inquire, "Why?" The answer depends largely on what one decides this "stuff" is. For centuries, both Jewish and Christian readers have attempted to interpret their way around the obvious by proposing that these poems are an allegory about God's love for the covenant people. (Christians often put the emphasis on Christ's love for his Church.) If this is the case, then the question of their belonging in the Bible is much easier to answer. God's love, after all, is a theme that runs like a river through both testaments.

What if, however, your teenager's instincts about these poems are correct? What if the Song of Solomon is "just an old-fashioned love song" between a man and a woman?

If this is the case it makes our "why is this stuff in the Bible" question a bit more difficult to answer. The rewards, however, may make the extra effort worthwhile.

Many Christians seem to forget that sex was God's idea in the first place. If we take the creation stories seriously, we must acknowledge this (even though we must also acknowledge that what God originally pronounced "good" is now subject to perversion and abuse through the Fall). The Song of Solomon reminds us that a man and woman's fully committed enjoyment of each other is itself a manifestation of God's extravagant mercy and grace.

Still we hesitate. Unable to accept the glorious good news of this unusual biblical book, we either avoid it altogether or spiritualize it into a less "offensive" form. Surely, there must be a more excellent way, especially in a world where sex is so grievously misunderstood.

Perhaps the first step in this "more excellent way" is to reexamine our views toward the material world in general. One modern parable that can help us do this is the movie *Babette's Feast*. It tells the story of a small, otherworldly sect bent on denying the pleasures of creation. When, by some ironic twist of providence, an accomplished French chef (Babette) ends up cooking the meal for the celebration of the sect's founder, the members are filled with apprehension. They meet secretly beforehand

and vow not to enjoy a morsel of it. "We will only use our tongues for prayer," they promise each other solemnly.

We can learn a lot from these people's pious but misguided determination. While tongues do work wonderfully well for prayer, we would be silly to deny the presence of God-given taste buds. Likewise, although the Song of Solomon works wonderfully well as an allegory of God's love for us, we would be silly to deny what it tells us about the God-given joys of human sexuality.

So we return to the question, Why is this stuff in the Bible? Maybe it is to remind us that God is the creator of human love, and the enjoyment of it is in a very real way the enjoyment of God. Thanks be to God for this miraculous gift!

FOR REFLECTION:

1. Is the Song of Solomon's celebration of human sexuality a license for promiscuity? Why or why not?

2. How does the Song of Solomon's portrayal of sex differ from the way sex is portrayed in popular culture?

3. Should we encourage young people to read these poems?

WHERE TWO OR THREE ARE GATHERED

Matthew 18:15–20

t is a sultry Sunday morning in mid-July. Church attendance is embarrassingly low. Half the congregation is on vacation, and the other half wishes they were. The minister, anxious to put a positive spin on the situation, greets the faithful remnant with these words from Matthew 18:20: "For where two or three are gathered in my name, I am there among them."

While I do not doubt the Holy Spirit's attendance at such occasions, I do wonder whether this verse really speaks to poorly attended church gatherings. After all, most have little to do with church discipline, which, believe it or not, is the context of this misunderstood verse from Matthew 18.

Have you ever been wronged by another church member? Has another Christian ever said or done something hurtful to you? Most of us with any church experience at all would probably answer "yes" to these questions. The more difficult question to answer is "What should we do about it?" That is the issue to which Matthew speaks in this neglected text.

Matthew outlines a three-step, "gentle but firm"

approach. First the individual should be approached privately. (No hypocritical back-stabbing allowed!) If this effort does not result in repentance, then one or two other church members should be brought along, presumably to add their persuasive powers to the task as well as to guard against its being one person's word against another. As a last resort, the person is to be brought before the church for further attempts at persuasion and reconciliation.

This is the point at which "gentle but firm" seems to turn into "harsh and unforgiving." Verse 17 counsels, "If the offender refuses to listen even to the church, let such a one be to you as a Gentile and a tax collector." Given that both Gentiles and tax collectors were shunned in Jewish society, this verdict seems to have the force of excommunication. The stamp of divine authority is placed on such decisions in verses 18–20, which reassure the church that whatever they "bind on earth will be bound in heaven" and that Jesus himself is present among even "two or three" who gather in his name.

We've come a long way from seeing verse 20 as a text for poorly attended church gatherings! If context is crucial for interpreting verse 20, however, it is also important for understanding this passage as a whole. Before we draw too many conclusions about its "harsh and unforgiving" bottom line, we ought to consider that context.

What does it mean to treat someone like a Gentile and a tax collector? Or more precisely, how did Jesus treat Gentiles and collectors?[8] According to Matthew, Jesus had a reputation for fraternizing with both. Jesus called a tax collector to be one of his disciples (Matt. 9:9). He was criticized by the Pharisees for dining with "many tax collectors and sinners" (Matt. 9:10–13). As for Gentiles, we could refer for starters to his healing of the Roman centurion's servant in Matthew 8:5–13, where Jesus sends the centurion home with the words "Go; let it be done for you according to your faith."

In short, Jesus' rule of thumb seems to have been that if a Gentile or a tax collector turned and came in faith, they were to be welcomed into fellowship and lavished with the same extravagant grace as everyone else! This puts rather a different spin on treating someone like a Gentile and a tax collector. If Jesus saw fit to leave room for repentance, those of us who gather in his name cannot afford to do less. Perhaps that is the most important lesson from this passage's context. Even if the church's doors must be closed to someone, they don't necessarily have to be locked.

FOR REFLECTION:

1. Is "church discipline" ever an issue in your congregation/denomination? If so, how is it handled?

2. What do you think of Matthew's "gentle but firm" approach? Would it work for you? Would it work for your church?

GOD'S STARTLING
SEATING CHART
Psalm 23:5

eating charts. They can mean the difference between festivity and fiasco, conviviality and calamity, pleasure and pain. Who of us, after all, wants to sit down to a sumptuous meal with our worst enemy? If it is true that "bad company ruins good morals," then it is surely also true that bad company ruins good dinner parties. Even the most savory dish tastes like sand when it is seasoned with tension and hostility.

This reality (which cannot be anything but constant over the course of the centuries) makes Psalm 23:5 very difficult to understand. I, for one, do not find the prospect of a table prepared for me "in the presence of my enemies" particularly inviting. Yet there it is. Sandwiched in among all the other comforting images of this beloved psalm is this metaphorical "clinker." The feast is spread before us, our cups are as bottomless as those in a child's magician kit. Yet the divine seating chart seems to have been fashioned expressly to spoil our fun. *Bon appetit?* Not a chance!

Is it any wonder that we tend to fast-forward through this phrase when we recite this familiar psalm? While it is true that the psalm as a whole occupies an unassailable spot in popular twentieth-century piety, it is almost certain that its popularity is not based on this puzzling verse. So in spite of the fact that we have been hearing it and saying it all our lives, there is a sense in which it still qualifies as a "neglected text."

Thirty-four centuries ago a group of princes wrote a letter to the Egyptian pharaoh then in power. In this letter they beg for the pharaoh to listen to them and to grant them gifts "while our enemies look on and eat dust." Their letter gives us an interesting insight into the ancient world, and Psalm 23:5. It suggests that there is an element of vindication in this image of the public reception of favor in the presence of one's enemies. The idea is that those who have opposed us—and the "lord" we represent—will be proven wrong and publicly shamed.[9]

It may seem difficult for Christians to reconcile this reading with Jesus' teaching about loving our enemies (Matt. 5:44). Yet the Bible has a place for this sort of public vindication, especially in cases where God's honor as well as our own is at stake. Isaiah 40:5, for instance, speaks to a situation in which God's people in exile are promised the return of their land and the restoration of God's favor. When these promises are fulfilled, Isaiah says, "then the glory of the Lord shall be revealed, *and all people shall see it together.*" Revelation 1:7, similarly, talks about that moment when Jesus Christ will return triumphant. His coming "with the clouds" ensures that "every eye will see him," even the eyes of "*those who pierced him.*" Both of these important passages seem to have an eye toward God's enemies. Part of their passion arises from the knowledge that God's name will not only be vindicated, but will be vindicated in the presence of the opposition.

Maybe this is why Psalm 23:3 talks about God's comfort and care being "for his name's sake." This is not to say that the Good Shepherd does not care about each and every one of His sheep. But it does caution us against reading this psalm as if it were only about *our* needs. The stakes are high for God here, too. And if we are at first a bit startled by the seating chart at the divine banquet, it will only be because our focus is too much on ourselves. Once we realize that God's honor is at stake, we will be able to celebrate the fact that the table is prepared where all our foes—and God's—can see.

FOR REFLECTION:

1. Had you ever noticed the phrase "in the presence of my enemies" in the psalm before? Had it bothered you? How had you interpreted it?

2. Whose side are you on? How do you know?

3. What situations make you long for the triumph of God?

A MESSAGE
FROM THE MARTYRS
Revelation 6:9–11

ome people interpret the book of Revelation as if it were so many tea leaves. Invariably, the verses converge at the bottom of their cups to reveal references to current political leaders and dire predictions of disaster. This approach to the book's interpretation has its devoted followers, of course, and for them the book is anything *but* a "neglected text." But for those Christians who are uncomfortable with such conjurings, the entire book often falls into disuse. Skittish about its misinterpretations, we dare not interpret it at all.

If Christians had a keener sense of Revelation as a book of comfort, we might not be so reluctant to read it. Penned in the context of persecution, John's vision of the consummation of Christ's kingdom seeks to reassure its readers that no matter how bad things get, God's justice will ultimately prevail.

Nowhere is this message more apparent than in Revelation 6:9–11. In these verses John describes the souls of the martyrs crying out for justice. "How long?" they plead with their Lord. "How long will it be before you judge and avenge our blood on the inhabitants of the earth?"

OK, so the comfort is not immediately obvious. Cries for vengeance rarely make twentieth-century Christians "comfort-able." If we try to hear this passage with first-century ears, however, it may sound a bit different. If you knew that you might be called upon to bear witness to your faith with your life, and more than that, through a horrible death, wouldn't this cry for vengeance sound forth from your heart as well? It is no coincidence that the Greek word for "witness" is *martus*, a term that even in the first century was well on its way to becoming the technical term "martyr." Christianity was a capital offense in those days, and many believers bore witness to it with their lives.

Now let's listen again for the comfort. Notice first where the martyrs are in John's picture of the heavenly Temple. They are depicted as being "under the altar" of God (v. 9). While this might strike us as being an undesirable place (like being "swept under the carpet" in modern parlance), there is, in fact, no place nearer to the heart of God for the ancient Christian. Picking up on Old Testament images of the altar as a place of sanctuary (see 1 Kings 1:49–53), this picture presents the martyrs as awaiting the resurrection in a place where no harm can possibly come to them. They are, literally, under the protection of the Most High God (see Ps. 84:3). The location also puts their deaths in the proper perspective. It reveals that their lives were not so much taken as *sacrificed*, that their blood was a symbol of life rather than death.

Neglected Texts

The martyrs' cry for vengeance has its comforting aspects as well (v. 10). The Greek word that is usually translated as "avenge" also means "procure justice for." It is justice the martyrs long for, justice for themselves and, by extension, for all who have suffered unjustly throughout the ages. The moment for which the martyrs long is the one for which we all long. It is that moment when the world will know that God is not some sort of absentee landlord, oblivious to all that is going on. The martyrs' cry reminds us that, in spite of all appearances, there will be a day when justice will "roll down like waters, and righteousness like an everflowing stream" (Amos 5:24).

It says something about the faith of these martyrs, I think, that they do not ask "whether" God's justice will win out, but "how long" it will be until it does. Even after enduring unspeakable horrors at the hands of their persecutors, they still bear witness to a God who is holy and true. This may be the most important message from the martyrs. In a world where murder no longer merits the front page, where the eyes of the innocents look out at us from the sides of milk cartons and cry "how long?" it is important for us to be reminded that God does not sit dispassionately by. If we ever needed proof of it, we need only look to Jesus Christ, the faithful witness (1:5), who mingled his own blood with that of the martyrs.

FOR REFLECTION:

1. Do you tend to ask "whether" God's justice will prevail, or "how long"?

2. Could you bear witness to your faith with your blood? Do you know anyone who has? How common is persecution in the modern world?

3. Respond to the statement: "The blood of the martyrs is the seed of the church."

YOU *CAN* GO HOME AGAIN

Jeremiah 31:7–14

ou Can't Go Home Again. Even if we haven't read Thomas Wolfe's novel, we know the truth of its title from bittersweet experience.

I suppose I was in college the first time I realized it, though goodness knows, I should have suspected sooner. It's just that I had been blessed to spend the first seventeen years of my life in one place. The faces around my family's dining room table stayed pretty much the same Sunday after Sunday. There were parents, grandparents, brothers, sisters, and often a full complement of cousins. When it got crowded my dad would simply make another leaf for the table, buying us enough elbow room to last until the next influx of babies and in-laws. So while the circle kept expanding, it remained, at least from my perspective, blissfully unbroken.

But then came college and the realization that I would never again have all of the people I loved in one place at one time. I had returned for the annual Thanksgiving orgy of family and food, only to discover that there were faces missing from the circle I defined as "home." Death had taken some, but distance had divided us as well.

Glimpses of Glory

To complicate matters further, I found that I also missed the new friends and surrogate family members I had collected at college. Would there ever be an occasion (aside from my funeral) that would bring them all together? I began to plot possible reunions, but in my heart I knew that even if everybody could come, I couldn't make it last.

Perhaps it was this experience—both bitter and sweet—that is behind my fascination with Jeremiah 31:7–14. Tucked into the beginning of a chapter made famous by its promises of a "new covenant" (vv. 31–34), this neglected text paints a picture of the homecoming for which we all long, the feast for which we all hunger. "See," Jeremiah writes on God's behalf, "I am going to bring them from the land of the north, and gather them from the farthest parts of the earth . . . With weeping they shall come and with consolations I will lead them back" (vv. 8a and 9a).

Oh, I know that originally this passage was written as an oracle of hope for the people of Israel, looking forward to the day when the exiles would return from Babylon (or perhaps even earlier from Assyria). But it would be a mistake, I think, to lock this passage's promises in the past. There is something about the extravagance of its imagery that continues to point toward the future, toward that day when all of God's wayward creation will gather from east and west and from north and south, to sit at a table in the kingdom of God.

Yet it is a humble kind of homecoming that Jeremiah pictures, both for Israel and for us. There is no ticker-tape parade waiting for Jeremiah's refugees. They come, not marching, but limping. The picture is not of battle-ready ranks, but of staggering sheep. The pace of their pilgrimage is set not by the strong, but by the weak—the blind, the lame, those who have just given birth, and those who are in the throes of labor. With shades of the Twenty-third Psalm, Jeremiah describes how the Shepherd will lead them gently along the brooks on straight, even paths in which they will not stumble.

But then the imagery shifts. Shepherd is revealed as Father—a father who ransoms his firstborn "from hands too strong for him" and throws a bountiful banquet in his honor. The faces of the guests reflect the radiance that comes with health and wholeness. The table groans under the weight of the grain, the wine, and the oil. The people are sated with God's goodness. Mourning gives way to dancing, and the sound of their song makes the mountains around the new Jerusalem ring. Best of all, however, is the promise of permanence. From now on, God vows, their lives will be like a watered garden, and they shall never languish again.

It is a powerful picture of home—the home toward which we all stagger—the table around which the circle will once again be unbroken.

Even a brief exposure to our culture's movie canon reveals how deep our own sense of homelessness is. The children's movie *The Land before Time* tells of a band of baby dinosaurs making their perilous way toward the "great valley" where families will be reunited and there will always be enough food. Or consider the more cynical version of this theme in the movie *The Trip to Bountiful*. It describes an elderly woman's struggles to return to her childhood home, only to find when she gets there that reality is starkly at odds with her memories. The moral of this story seems to be very much along the lines of Thomas Wolfe's title: *You Can't Go Home Again*.

For a culture obsessed with a longing for home but cynical about our ability to get there, scripture's good news is as good as it gets. Jeremiah 31 bears witness to a God who is determined to bring us back to the garden, the table, and home. The Gospels pick up where Jeremiah leaves off, telling of the lengths to which God is prepared to go to ransom us "from hands too strong" for us. Hear the good news: you *can* go home again!

FOR REFLECTION:

1. When did you first realize that you would never have all the people you loved in one place at one time? Or have you realized it?

2. How do you picture heaven? Is Jeremiah's vision anything like yours? Is heaven more than just a big family reunion?

CONVERSATIONS THROUGH THE SCREEN DOOR

Luke 1:26–38

t is a day like any other day in Nazareth, or at least it is until the angel Gabriel shows up. Mary hears the doorbell and, mindful of her parents' warnings, decides to size up the stranger through the safety of the locked screen door. Gabriel tries to put her at ease with his opening line: "Greetings, favored one! The Lord is with you!" Mary remains skeptical, however, and wonders to herself "what sort of greeting this might be." But nothing could have prepared her for his next announcement. She is pregnant, he says. And what's more, her unborn son will be the "Son of the Most High."

If Gabriel had expected the young woman to be overwhelmed with this information, he had forgotten to reckon with her incredible poise and practicality. "How can this be," she replies warily, "since I am a virgin?"

Gabriel's answer is the only one with a prayer of breaching Mary's defenses. And as far out as it sounds, it makes a certain exhilarating sense to this young Jewish woman. "The Holy Spirit will come upon you," Gabriel explains, "and the power of the Most High will overshadow you." Spirit. Holy Spirit. Echoes begin to reverberate in Mary's mind. In her language it can also mean "wind" or "breath." And it is a word she has heard since before she can remember. It is from the opening verses of the Torah: "the earth was without form and void, and darkness was upon the face of the deep; and the Spirit of God was moving over the face of the waters" (Gen. 1:2, RSV). Perhaps this stranger is serious, Mary muses. After all, the Spirit who created all life is certainly capable of creating one small life.

Sensing from the expression on her face that he is making headway, Gabriel follows up with an illustration. Her cousin Elizabeth is also pregnant, he announces. She is six months along, in fact, in spite of her age and previous inability to bear children. "So you see," Gabriel adds gently, "nothing shall be impossible with God."

There is a moment of charged silence as Mary considers her response. At last, her hand moves to unlock the door, and she hears herself saying the words that will change her life forever: "Here am I, the servant of the Lord; let it be with me according to your word."

We can never be sure exactly what Mary was thinking on that day in Nazareth. Nor can we know for certain just what it was that moved her from skepticism to submission. But in this contemporized retelling of the story, I hope we can begin to see some of the things that have slipped into the shadows in our reading of this familiar text. We have read it so often that we have read right over the story's own hints about Mary's initial resistance to the "good news" of her pregnancy. The often neglected details of this passage reveal a Mary who shows remarkable presence of mind under pressure. She is strong, smart, and really rather savvy! These aspects of her character are critical if we are to appreciate the significance of her submissive response at the end of the story.

Submission is seriously out of vogue in today's culture. There are some good reasons for this. Women, particularly, are sensitive to the ways in which biblical injunctions to "submit" have been used and abused throughout history. Yet the kind of submission Mary models in this passage is a powerful example for all Christians, male and female. Mary's story reminds us that submission to God is anything *but* passive. As Presbyterian pastor Karen Pidcock-Lester once said,

> When we submit all that we have, all that we are, and all that we hold dear to the God who is Lord of all, it is a strong and beautiful thing. Indeed, it may be the hardest thing we ever do.[10]

HAPPY ALL THE TIME?
Philippians 4:1–7

ost of my childhood memories of church involve singing. Sunday school was my favorite precisely because it always began with fifteen minutes of what, from a musical standpoint, could only have been called "joyful noise." One of the songs we sang with particular gusto went like this:

> Since Jesus Christ came in
>   and cleansed my heart from sin
> I'm inright, outright, upright, downright
>   happy all the time.

The pointing actions that accompanied "inright, outright, upright, downright" were, of course, the song's primary appeal. Beyond that, however, its attraction began to fade for me. Even as a child I can remember feeling vaguely disturbed by the song's grandiose theological claims. Are Christians really supposed to be happy *all the time*? If I wasn't, did that mean I wasn't a good Christian?

Similar questions might well confront the reader of Philippians 4:4. At first glance Paul's admonition to "rejoice in the Lord always" seems as naive as the words of

that Sunday school song. "Get real," we are tempted to re-
tort. "Keep your Pollyanna piety. Come back and talk to
us when you decide to live in the real world."

While our reaction is understandable, it is manifestly
unfair to Paul. A closer look at the oft-neglected context
of this verse reveals that Paul's world was every bit as real
as our own.

Our first clue comes in the verses just prior to Paul's
"hymn to joy." Verses 2 and 3 put a positive slant on
what was obviously a negative situation in the Philippian church. Two women, Euodia and Syntyche, are
urged to "be of the same mind." Another unnamed
"loyal companion" is encouraged to help them along in
this endeavor. The need for conflict management and
resolution in the church is, evidently, not a modern phe-
nomenon!

Internal dissension was the least of the Philippian
church's problems, however. Though the exact nature of
the threat is unclear, other parts of Paul's letter hint that
his favorite flock was being threatened from without as
well as within (see 1:28–29 and 3:2). Paul knew that if
they were going to survive such attacks, they were going
to have to present a united front, "standing firm in one
spirit, striving side by side with one mind for the faith of
the gospel" (1:27).

Paul's own personal context is the most telling, however. His injunction to rejoice is written from prison. One
gets the impression that he expects to be executed at any
time. Yet danger does not diminish his joy. He can speak
of his death and his joy in the same breath (2:17–18).
When he urges the troubled Philippian church to rejoice,

he does so knowing that joy is often something Christians do *in spite of* rather than *because of.*

Lewis Smedes is tuned in to this kind of joy when he observes that "joy is possible even when pleasure turns to ashes."[11] For the Christian, joy is not dependent on external circumstances. It is not grounded in the ephemeral "pursuit of happiness," but in the abiding assurance that "we belong, body and soul, to our faithful Savior, Jesus Christ" (Heidelberg Catechism, Q & A #1).

It was this kind of joy that a young pastor encountered when he entered the hospital room of an elderly saint named Edith.[12] It was the last day of Edith's life; the pastor knew it and so did Edith. So when he asked her, "How are you?" they both knew that he was talking about more than her health. Their eyes locked, and she answered with a serenity born of both suffering and grace: "I have never felt such pain, or known more joy."

Are Christians happy all the time? No, of course not. But they can be joyful all the time. Theirs is a joy that flows directly from the fountain of God's amazing grace, a joy that, like God's peace, "passes all understanding" (4:7).

FOR REFLECTION:

1. How does the pursuit of happiness differ from the pursuit of joy?

2. Who is the most profoundly joyful Christian you know? How do they express that joy? How do they affect those around them?

THE TRAGEDY OF TAMAR
2 Samuel 13:1–19

he story of the rape of Tamar is so unsettling that it does not even make it into the common lectionary. Evidently the people who put together those lists of preachable passages do not consider it appropriate fare for Sunday morning. And to be honest, the wise preacher might want to preface this reading with a "PG-13" rating. In turning our eyes away from Tamar's tragic story, however, we risk missing out on an important message about the abuse of power, the violation of trust, and the communal character of sin.

The story begins innocently enough. Amnon has fallen hard for his half sister, Tamar. Their close family ties do not seem to be an issue in the story; such a match would not have violated any taboos at that time. More relevant than their being related to each other is the fact that they are related to King David, who is their father. Amnon is first in line for the throne; Tamar's full brother, Absalom, is a close second. This tips us off from the outset that whatever happens, the risks are high. The stability of the kingdom may well be at stake.

As time passes, Amnon's lovesick state attracts the

attention of the wily Jonadab, who suggests a plan for luring Tamar into Amnon's private chamber. This is the point at which the story starts to turn sinister. Up until now we have been able to sympathize with Amnon's plight. As the plot unfolds, however, we realize with sickening surety that unrequited love has mutated into unrelenting lust.

In obedience to their father David's orders, Tamar goes to Amnon's house to bake him some of his favorite cakes. She performs this mission of mercy in the courtyard—well inside the dictates of propriety, and well outside the reach of her half brother's bedroom. Amnon, however, will only eat from her hand, and in complete privacy at that.

It is interesting that the story has not recorded a single word of Tamar's up to this point. She speaks volumes, however, in her brief, pointed reply to her half brother's suggestion that they have sex. Her response is remarkable under the circumstances. With firmness, diplomacy, and poise she points out that such behavior would be "vile" and would leave her in disgrace. She suggests that he simply approach their father and ask permission to marry her. Though it reveals nothing about how Tamar actually feels, this remark does demonstrate her presence of mind. She has, after all, managed to say "No" without insulting her attacker.

But reason does not work. The Bible goes out of its way to discourage blaming the victim in the way that it describes the actual rape. It says, "But he would not listen to her, and being stronger than she, he forced her and lay with her" (v. 14).

The next part of the story would be utterly inexplicable if it were not for the unpredictability of human nature and the bitterness of wounded pride. Immediately after the rape, Amnon "was seized with a very great loathing" for his victim, a loathing, the Bible says, even greater than his previous lust. So he speaks but two terse words to her: "Get out." To his manservant he commands, "Put this woman out of my presence and bolt the door after her" (v. 17).

Tamar's prediction of the consequences of Amnon's foolishness turns out to be brutally accurate. Tamar, we are told, dwelt as "a desolate woman in her brother Absalom's house" (v. 20). This would probably have been her only recourse in a society that had no respectable place for women who were neither virgins nor wives.

The complex character of sin really shows itself in the aftermath of Amnon's act. Tamar's brother Absalom eventually avenges his sister's disgrace and kills Amnon. This act in turn breeds more disgrace and estrangement until, at last, Absalom's story ends in death as well.

Sin is complicated business. What started as a story about unrequited love ends up looking more like the St. Valentine's Day Massacre. And the carnage does not end on the individual level. In retrospect we realize that the entire course of Israel's history took an irrevocable turn when love turned to lust and a brother violated his sister's and his society's trust.

Nineteenth-century novelist George Eliot once wrote this about sin: "Our deeds," she said, "carry their terrible consequences . . . consequences that are hardly ever confined to ourselves."[13] Tamar's story reads like a case study in the communal character of sin. Its consequences reach like tentacles across countless innocent lives and generations. And while it makes for depressing reading, it is important reading nonetheless. Until we can come to grips with the awful complexity of sin, we can never fully appreciate God's act of love for us in Jesus Christ. We can never fully appreciate the magnitude of the claim that 2 Corinthians 5:21 makes: that for our sake God "made him to be sin who knew no sin, so that in him we might become the righteousness of God."

As for the Tamars of this world, there is little one can say that will not sound sanctimonious. Yet maybe we could venture this much: There *is* a place where you can "carry your shame" (v. 13). It is to the one who knows what it means to be a victim, to the one who says, "See, I am making all things new" (Rev. 21:5).

FOR REFLECTION:

1. Are you glad this story is in the Bible? Why or why not?

2. Read 2 Samuel 14:27. Is there some hope here? Is it enough?

3. Are the consequences of our sins ever confined to ourselves? Back up your answer with examples.

SWEATING THE DETAILS
John 20:1-18

he resurrection of Jesus Christ is mostly a matter of faith. At the end of the day, you either believe it or you don't. The gospel writers knew this. Scattered throughout their accounts of that first Easter morning, however, are details that, precisely because of their ordinariness, lend authenticity to their stories. John's apparently offhand reference to the cloth from Jesus' face is one of these.

In John's version of the story, Mary Magdalene comes to the tomb first. Though it is still dark when she arrives, one thing is appallingly clear to her: Jesus' tomb has been tampered with. Mary seems to lay the blame with grave robbers. She runs back with the anguished report that "they have taken the Lord out of the tomb, and we do not know where they have laid him" (v. 2).

Peter and John race to the tomb to substantiate her story. John gets there first. Apparently, the sun has risen sufficiently for him to see into the tomb when he bends down to peer in through the low doorway. He sees the linen wrappings in which Jesus had been buried lying there discarded. In other words, he sees nothing that would lead him to doubt Mary's initial explanation for the tomb's desecration.

When Peter arrives, probably gasping for breath, he rushes past his cautious colleague and storms straight into the tomb. Again, the gospel writer repeats the detail of the linen grave cloths, but then adds that "the cloth that had been on Jesus' head [was] not lying with the linen wrappings but rolled up in a place by itself" (v.7). John finally musters the courage to go in. And then, the Bible says matter-of-factly, "he saw and believed" (v. 8). But wait, says the wondering reader. What did he believe, and why did he believe it only after going into the tomb?

One could conclude that John simply believed Mary's original explanation: grave robbers were responsible for the disappearance of Jesus' body. (Such was, evidently, a common enough occurrence at that time.) Two things, however, argue against that interpretation. First, he had had enough information for that kind of belief before he actually entered the tomb. The dislodged stone and the discarded wrappings would only have substantiated Mary's theory. Second, the Bible itself refers to Jesus' resurrection right after this statement that John "saw and believed" (v. 9). This seems to imply that his "belief" was in an alternate, and wholly unexpected, explanation for the empty tomb.

So what made the difference? What moved John from anguished doubt to electrifying faith? The easiest and best answer is probably "God's Spirit." Yet one wonders if the Spirit didn't drop a few hints along the way.

In the Bible one does not often find details lying around loose, just thrown in for fun or local color. So our attention is immediately drawn to this detail of the cloth from Jesus' face, "rolled up in a place by itself." It was, evidently, only observable from inside the tomb, since the Bible only makes mention of it when Peter actually goes inside. Could this have been what made the difference for John, or at least set him searching for an alternate explanation?

If you were a grave robber, would you take the time in a dark and dangerous situation to roll up and set aside the cloth on the face of the corpse? Somehow I doubt it. Perhaps John doubted it, too. Perhaps it was that very detail that didn't ring true with the grave robber theory. Perhaps the picture in that empty tomb was not one of haste and guilty stealth, but one of a risen Lord, calmly sitting up, stretching as if from sleep, and rolling up the cloth that had fallen from his face.

We will never know, of course, whether this tantalizing detail was what turned faith's tide for John. There it is, however, preserved for the centuries in the gospel account, inviting both believers and doubters throughout the ages to "sweat the details."

FOR REFLECTION:

1. Had you noticed the detail about the cloth before? Does it make any difference in your view of the resurrection?

2. If someone told you that he or she had scientific evidence for or against the resurrection, would you believe it? Would you want to hear the evidence?

BIBLE
PORTRAITS

HANNAH
AND HER SISTERS
1 Samuel 1:1–20

"asn't that a wonderful Mother's Day sermon?" the well-meaning woman asked her young female friend as they sipped coffee in the fellowship hall. There was no answer. Nor would there be. Her friend had set her cup down with a clatter and run toward the women's room in tears.

Mother's Day is notoriously tough on "women in waiting," that is, those who are trying desperately—and unsuccessfully—for a child. They and their husbands mark time by the rhythm of monthly disappointments. Mother's Day often heightens their sense of failure and loss. Insensitive friends—and preachers—often unintentionally spill salt in the wound by acting as if becoming a parent were as simple as placing an order from a catalogue!

Hannah would have understood about the salt. Except in her case, the spill was no accident. Peninnah knew full well what she was doing when she aimed her salty taunts at Elkanah's other wife. She wanted her rival to feel every humiliating grain. So year after year Peninnah found opportunities to remind Hannah that, while Hannah might have Elkanah's love, Peninnah had his children.

Glimpses of Glory

Today, a woman's worth is no longer measured by how many children she has. (Or at least, it shouldn't be!) Though barrenness is not the disgrace it once was, however, women are often asked to account for their childlessness. And for those who want children but cannot have them, the social sting can smart almost as badly as it did in Hannah's day.

If misery loves company, then Hannah must have taken some comfort from all of her biblical sisters who endured the same waiting game. Three of the four matriarchs had difficulty conceiving (Sarah, Rebekah, and Rachel). Samson's mother had been pronounced barren as well. And if we look to the New Testament, Elizabeth, the mother of John the Baptist, joins the list. Hannah, it seems, had many sisters!

Part of these stories' appeal may lie in the importance of the births they narrate. Their "baby roll" is impressive: Isaac, Jacob, Joseph, Samson, Samuel, John the Baptist. . . . In other words, part of the way these stories function is to underscore the grace of God. They are case studies in close calls, making us realize how close we came *not* to having these crucial characters in salvation history's all-star cast. Yet one wonders if the stories of Hannah and her sisters may not function on a more personal level as well.

A childless friend of mine once confided that she had read Hannah's story every month for the ten years she and her husband had been trying to conceive a child. When I asked her why, she gave three reasons. First, she identified strongly with Hannah's longing for a child. Second, she appreciated what Hannah must have felt when others tormented her about her childlessness. And finally, it reminded her that God does care about her pain. Just the fact that the story is there, preserved in our scriptures, bears witness to the fact that God does hear and understand, and that God will, somehow, remember.

My only concern for my friend is that she might mistakenly come away from this story with the feeling that she and her husband just haven't prayed hard enough. While Hannah's story does end happily, we ought not to use it to compound the anguish of women and men who have prayed—and are still praying—with sighs too deep for words. Goodness knows, they already have enough salt in their wounds!

Why doesn't God answer their prayers in the affirmative? The simple answer is that no one knows. Even the Bible doesn't speculate on this and only rarely gives the reasons for the "opening" or "closing" of someone's womb. Yet one thing is abundantly clear: the birth of a child is a gift of God's grace.

Maybe we should take our cue from that grace on Mother's Day. Our children are gifts, not merit badges. As we "rejoice with those who rejoice," let us not forget to "weep with those who weep" (Rom. 12:15). Let us not forget Hannah and all of her sisters.

FOR REFLECTION:

1. In what ways do you identify with Hannah's story? What does her story teach us about children? About waiting? About prayer?

2. How can Christians celebrate Mother's Day and Father's Day more sensitively?

THE CALL OF DUTY

Jonah 1

as God ever called you to a place you did not want to go? To a task you did not want to do? To words you did not want to say?

This is the presenting problem in the book of Jonah. God points in one direction and Jonah goes the other. Jonah's reaction is so abrupt that it catches us completely off guard. A mild but eloquent protest would be one thing—something, say, along the lines of Jeremiah's objections about being too young, or Moses' claim that he wasn't much of a public speaker. But a trip to the travel agent? Jonah's reaction is so extreme that it borders on the ridiculous.

Most of us are pretty good at rationalizing our disobedience. Jonah, too, had his reasons. The content of God's call was enough to make further explanations unnecessary. He was being asked to preach repentance to Nineveh, the archenemy of his people. Nineveh was the capitol of the nation that would eventually sweep like a scourge through the nation of Israel to carry its people off into captivity. Small wonder Jonah could think of better places to go!

Still, if it had been simply a matter of lofting a little fire and brimstone over the walls of Nineveh, Jonah might not have objected so strongly. The real reason for his reluctance comes out in chapter 4. There he confesses—after Nineveh's conversion—that this was the very thing he'd been afraid of. When God had shown *mercy* to the enemy, Jonah's deepest fears had been realized. Heaven forbid that God should be gracious to anyone but the chosen people!

Jonah was not ready for the hard theological lesson God had in store for him. It flew in the face of the narrow exclusivism of his age. That God might possibly love outside of Israel's borders, that God might possibly act in a way that was contrary to his own rigid notions of the faith, was not just unpalatable for Jonah, it was unthinkable.

We, too, often have good reasons for avoiding God's proddings. Yet divine duty has a way of running roughshod over our carefully contrived rationalizations. When push comes to shove, we must come to terms with the fact that the Christian life is not about the pursuit of our own happiness. God often asks us to do things that make us uncomfortable.

In a nineteenth-century novel by George Eliot, a young woman named Romola receives a talking-to from a passing priest. She, like Jonah, is on her way out of town. And like Jonah, she is following the inclinations of her heart rather than the call of divinely appointed duty. The priest's words to her are a reminder for all of us who have travelled that same road. He says,

> You are seeking your own will my daughter . . . But how will you find good? It is not a thing of choice: it is a river

that flows from the foot of the Invisible Throne, and flows by the path of obedience. I say again, man cannot choose his duties. You may choose to forsake your duties, and choose not to have the sorrow they bring. But you will go forth; and what will you find, my daughter? Sorrow without duty—bitter herbs, and no bread with them.[14]

What is the call of duty in your life? Is it God's call? Are you trying to avoid it?

These are questions that no one can answer for us. The answers must be sought through suffering, struggle, and prayer. As we seek them, however, we need to remember that the Bible's path to "personal fulfillment" often leads in a very different direction than the world's. It may not be a comfortable path. It may even lead to a cross. Yet it runs by the river that flows from the foot of the Invisible Throne. And it is the only path to peace, the only path to joy.

FOR REFLECTION:

1. Has God ever called you to a place you did not want to go? To a task you did not want to do? To words you did not want to say? How did you react?

2. What is the call of duty in your life? Is it God's call? Are you trying to avoid it?

3. How do we discern our Christian duty, both as individuals and as a community of faith?

JEZEBEL:
BAD GIRL OF THE BIBLE
1 Kings 21

ezebel's reputation is so bad that her name has become synonymous with wickedness. Even the dictionary describes a "jezebel" as an "impudent or shameless woman." In most people's minds she reigns unrivaled as the "bad girl" of the Bible.

Popular impressions of her character (or lack of it) do have some basis in the Bible. In the book of Revelation the name is given to a false prophetess who seduces unsuspecting believers into sexual and religious promiscuity (Rev. 2:20–23). In the Old Testament, however, Jezebel's sins are portrayed in less sexual terms.

For the Old Testament authors, the biggest strike against Jezebel is that she is a foreigner, and a Baal-worshiper at that. Indeed, she approaches her religion with murderous zeal, attempting to "neutralize" all of Israel's prophets (see 1 Kings 18 and 19). Yet, however much the Old Testament authors love to hate her, they do not try to cover up Jezebel's strength and cleverness. Nowhere is this more obvious than in 1 Kings 21, where her take-charge attitude is an important part of the point.

The chapter opens innocently enough. Jezebel's husband, King Ahab, puts an offer on some property adjacent to the couple's royal residence in Jezreel. It seems a reasonable offer, since Ahab proposes to pay good money for the vineyard, or if the owner prefers, to exchange it for property that is even more prime.

There is only one problem. Naboth, the owner of the vineyard, won't sell. Unless we read carefully, we are likely to misread his motivation. The key is in the wording of his refusal. "The LORD forbid that I should give you my ancestral inheritance," he says in verse 3. In other words, it isn't just any old vineyard, but part of what his family has held in trust since the time of the conquest. Selling it would be like selling the family Bible that came over on the boat, the one with all the ancestral records inscribed at the front. It is unthinkable. The very idea that one could put a price tag on it is an insult.

Ahab does not seem to understand this. With behavior reminiscent of a five-year-old, he storms back to the palace, flings himself across his bed, and refuses to eat.

Enter Jezebel. Evidently Ahab's antics have gotten her attention (isn't that what most five-year-olds are after?). She asks him what's wrong. He tells her but neglects to mention the part about the vineyards being part of Naboth's inheritance. Jezebel's next question is a loaded one. "Do you now govern Israel?" she asks. Given what happens next, it's not clear that he does.

When Jezebel says "Jump!" her servants ask, "How high?" She spits out a series of orders designed to eliminate Naboth through the very law that he loves. False witnesses are procured to accuse Naboth of both blasphemy and sedition. The penalty—conveniently—is death. The execution is hardly over before the "For Sale" sign goes up at Naboth's family vineyard.

Once our heads stop spinning, we may pause to marvel at the fact that a Phoenician princess would know enough about Israelite law to carry off such a conspiracy. Yet that knowledge may be an important part of this story's point. It is not enough, after all, to know the law. We must also follow it. The biblical author uses Jezebel as a scalding illustration of the scandal of knowledge without obedience.

The end of Jezebel's story is equally instructive (see 2 Kings 9:30–37). Ever concerned with appearances, Jezebel touches up her makeup just before being hurled out of a window to her death. God, evidently, is not fooled by appearances.

As Christians we would do well to remember Jezebel's story. Just as readers recognize the obscenity of her actions, non-Christians are quick to see the inconsistency of Christians who are all form and no substance. Jesus' words about "whited sepulchers" come to mind. Whether we are active scofflaws (like Jezebel) or passive ones (like Ahab), the contradiction is equally destructive to our Christian witness.

FOR REFLECTION:

1. Do you have any sympathy for Jezebel at all? Why or why not? Does she have any traits that our modern world admires?

2. Think of a situation in which you have known what was right but did not act on it. What was the result, both for you and for others?

A CRISIS OF FAITH:
SARAI'S STORY

Genesis 16

"  romises, promises. . . . " So must Sarai have thought when her husband Abram came back into the tent that night after stargazing with God. "Look toward the heaven and count the stars," God had said to the eager Abram. "So shall your descendants be" (Gen. 15:5).

She had heard it all before. God had been making promises like that for years now. But here they both were, well into their eighties and not getting any younger. Whom was God kidding?

The worst part was that she felt particularly responsible. She was the one who was barren (Gen. 11:30). In the back of her mind she wondered whether that was why Abram had seemed so nonchalant during that awkward Egyptian incident several years before (see Gen. 12:10–20). If the Pharaoh had appropriated her as a permanent part of his harem, Abram could have traded her in for a new, more fertile wife. But as providence would have it (why, she wondered?), she had been rescued from the Pharaoh's house and reinstated in her role as Roadblock to the Promise.

Desperate times call for desperate measures. That was

what she told herself when she suggested the surrogacy scheme (Gen. 16:1–2). After all, it was common enough for a childless woman to give her slave girl to her husband as a means of obtaining the children she could not have with her own body. Thus, Hagar was sent. Abram seemed agreeable enough.

We will never know, of course, if these were precisely Sarai's sentiments as she reflected on the plan that was to be the cause of so much anguish and strife. Yet the Bible tells us enough to know that the plan was not proposed lightly. They had been in Canaan for ten years, after all (v.3), and there was nothing to show for God's progeny promise. The pressure must have been incredible, especially in a culture that blamed infertility on the woman.

What most commentators fail to see in this story, however, is Sarai's crisis of faith. She believed, after all, that if she was barren, it was because God had "closed her womb" (see Gen. 20:17–18; 30:2). What was God playing at, then, making all these promises?

There is a sense in which Sarai's act of desperation can be seen as an act of faith, and a selfless one at that. There were, after all, risks involved. And even if Sarai had not fully anticipated Hagar's subsequent behavior, it could not have been pleasant to send someone else in to have sex with one's husband. Perhaps she reasoned that God had been waiting for just such an act of selflessness, testing her to see if she was willing to sacrifice something of herself for the fulfillment of the promise.

In hindsight, of course, it was a terrible mistake. The

child of Hagar and Abram's union was not the child of the promise. That was a role reserved for Isaac, the son born miraculously to Sarah and Abraham (now with new names to celebrate their new identities) in chapter 21. Yet God was still able to find enough grace in the overflow to take care of Hagar and her son Ishmael, promising them a heritage of their own.

The moral of Sarai's story is not that she was a bad or unbelieving person. Rather, it is a story of a woman who lost patience with God, and who forgot that nothing is "too wonderful for the LORD" (Gen. 18:14). Her misguided act of faith illustrates both the dangers of trying to force God's hand and God's own capacity to redeem our mistakes.

This was not the last time that Sarah and Abraham would come up against situations in which reality seemed to fly in the face of God's promises. Perhaps the worst was when God asked Abraham to sacrifice the very child for whom they had waited so long (Gen. 22). John Calvin's comments on that story offer encouragement and counsel to all of us who find ourselves caught in such crises of faith:

> In such straits, the only remedy against despondency is, to leave the event to God, in order that he may open a way for us where there is none. For as we act unjustly towards God, when we hope for nothing from him but what our senses can perceive, so we pay Him the highest honor, when, in affairs of perplexity, we nevertheless entirely acquiesce in his providence.[15]

ANDREW:
SERVANT IN THE SHADOWS
John 1:35–42

ost of us would be hard pressed to remember much about the apostle Andrew. We all remember stories about his famous brother Simon Peter—the Big Fisherman, the Rock on which Jesus said he would build his Church, the disciple who denied Jesus three times. But Andrew? Confronted with a quiz-show-style question about Andrew, most of us would stammer, "Andrew who?"

Our stunning loss of memory may not be entirely our fault. In the gospels themselves the figure of Peter looms so large that Andrew tends to get lost in his brother's shadow. Even the story of Andrew's recognition of Jesus as the Messiah in John 1:35–42 reads like an introduction to Peter's first encounter with the Christ. Yet if we look carefully at this story, we can learn a lot from the little it tells us about Andrew.

Andrew started out as a disciple of John the Baptist (vv. 35, 40). From that we can conclude a few things about him. First, we know that he was a Jew, but a Jew who was not so focused on the past as to be blind to what God was doing in the present. He was a listener, a thinker, a man open to change. These were the qualities that enabled him to hear and follow the voice of John the Baptist crying in the wilderness. More importantly, these were the qualities that enabled him to recognize the Lamb of God.

What Andrew did after that recognition is even more revealing. After ascertaining where Jesus was staying, he went straight to find his brother, Simon. Once he found him, he did not mince words. "We have found the Messiah!" he announced bluntly. We are not told what Simon's reaction was, only that Andrew "brought Simon to Jesus" (v. 42). The rest, as they say, was history.

One wonders whether it ever occurred to Andrew not to tell Simon. After all, he'd grown up with him. He knew of his dynamic personality, his charisma, his gift for leadership. He must have known that with Simon as a fellow disciple he would quickly recede into the big man's shadow. But the Bible does not tell us what Andrew thought. It only tells us what he did. And what he did was not the act of an ambitious man or a selfish man—just a man who recognized the Savior of the world and wanted to spread the Good News.

I wonder how many Christians go through life thinking of themselves as living in the shadow of other Christians whose work for Christ is more obvious than theirs. How many Christians assume that their work for God is somehow less important, second class, just because they don't preach sermons, or do crusades on national television, or write books about faith. The story of Andrew belies that kind of logic. While he may have lived in the shadow of "the Rock," it's what he did in that shadow that was important. He used the gifts God gave him for listening, for recognition, for selflessness. Because he did, he influenced the whole Christian church.

I will never forget the last time I talked with my Aunt Grace, another of God's servants in the shadows. At age 102, Grace (appropriately named), was living in a nursing home. It took her a moment to recognize which of her several great-nieces I was. But she did figure it out. Once she did, she not only knew *who* I was but *how old* I was. I asked her how she kept her mind so sharp. She replied matter-of-factly, "I pray for all my relatives every day." Pretty impressive, especially when one considers that the list of *immediate* family members alone totaled 119. And knowing my Aunt Grace, I don't doubt that she prayed for some nonrelatives as well.

The stories of both Grace and Andrew remind us that one doesn't have to be in the limelight to serve the Savior. In the last analysis, it is not visibility that determines the value of our service to God but rather the way we carry out the job that God assigns to each of us, whether we be "butcher, or baker, or cabinet maker." True Christian vocation is service rendered not for recognition, but for the greater glory of God. Even if we do serve in the shadows, we can take comfort in the knowledge that even the darkness is as light to Thee (Ps. 139:12).

FOR REFLECTION:

1. Are you an Andrew or a Peter? Do you think you would have acted as Andrew did?

2. Have you ever resented a lack of recognition for service in the church? How do you feel about those who receive more recognition?

3. If service is not really about recognition, should we recognize gifts of service at all? Why or why not?

MRS. JOB:
A WOMAN OF FEW WORDS
Job 2

he sliver was a wicked one. It was deeply embedded in our six-year-old daughter's index finger. The moment of truth had arrived (though only after we flushed her out of her hiding place behind the hedge). Ellen now sat constrained on her father's lap, while I stood poised beside them with the tweezers.

The operation commenced, a fact of which our entire neighborhood must have been aware. After several seconds of incoherent screaming (it seemed like longer), our daughter wailed, "I want my mommy!"

My husband and I exchanged stress-laden smiles. "You've got her, honey," I said, wielding the tweezers.

Ellen gulped for air and tried again. "I want my daddy!"

"I'm afraid I'm in on this, too," said her father, grimly. Ellen's stunned silence was but the calm before the storm.

Betrayal. A sense of utter and absolute betrayal was, I suspect, what fed Ellen's screams the most at that moment. Never mind that we had patiently explained the necessity of removing the sliver. For her, the reality of the tweezers loomed larger than logic. That it was her mother who wielded them made it exponentially worse.

Job's wife (we don't, unfortunately, know her name), knew the feeling. When she and her husband lost everything as a result of a cosmic bet (see Job 1), she discovered what it was like to receive pain from the one who had previously been her primary source of strength and consolation. Of course, she did not *know* about the wager between God and "the Satan" (in Hebrew the name simply means "the accuser"). From her limited perspective, disaster had struck like an undeserved bolt from the blue. In a day when suffering was widely seen as punishment for sin, it made little sense to the wife of a man renowned for his righteousness.

Biblical commentators are notoriously unsympathetic when Mrs. Job counsels her husband to "Curse God and die" (Job 2:9). They like to fuss and fume about her lack of faith. And of course, they contrast her attitude with the "patience" of her husband, who refuses to take her advice. (Job is, by the way, much *less* patient in subsequent chapters!)

What the commentators forget is that Mrs. Job is operating with a lot less information than they are. They, along with the rest of the readers of the book, are privy to the scene in God's heavenly throne room. That scene offers us something very rare in both Scripture and life: a clear (albeit troubling) explanation for a particular person's suffering. In real life we walk around—to borrow a phrase from George Eliot—"well-wadded in stupidity," never sure precisely what our suffering is about.[16]

If we put ourselves in Mrs. Job's shoes for a moment we can begin to understand her attitude. (We may also see that she has grasped the theological dilemma better than the commentators do!) She knows better than anyone that her husband is a good man. She does not even consider "sin" as an explanation for what has happened to him (in contrast to Job's "friends" later in the book). From Mrs. Job's perspective, there can only be one explanation for what has happened: God is unjust. And a god who is unjust is no god at all. Hence her famous few words: "curse God and die." What other choice is there?

Job himself illustrates that there *is* another choice. He persists in his faith, confident that God's goodness will eventually "out." Yet his struggle is not pretty. The rest of the book of Job is reminiscent of another anguished accusation quoted from the cross: "My God, my God, why have you forsaken me?" (Ps. 22:1).

After the death of his wife, Joy, C. S. Lewis accused God of being little more than a "Cosmic Sadist."[17] That a Christian of Lewis's caliber could entertain such thoughts is comforting in its way. It puts him in the company of Job, Mrs. Job, and all the rest of us who walk around well-wadded in stupidity. Yet perhaps the following words are the ones that are, after all, the most profound. After Lewis had gained a bit more perspective on his loss he reflected: "You can't see anything properly while your eyes are blurred with tears."[18]

My daughter Ellen would agree. And so, we hope, would Mrs. Job.

FOR REFLECTION:

1. To what extent can we understand why we suffer?

2. Have you ever been in a situation that made you want to "curse God and die"? Does it look any different in retrospect?

GUESS WHO'S COMING TO DINNER?

Luke 10:38–42

ith whom do you identify when you read Luke 10:38–42? Is it Mary, the sister who sits quietly at Jesus' feet, drinking in his every word? Or Martha, the sister who is "distracted with much serving" and resents her sister's absence from the kitchen?

I used to side squarely with Mary. Looking back on it, I suspect this had something to do with the fact that Martha reminded me of my older sister. To be honest, my conveniently timed absences from the kitchen were often motivated more by laziness than a genuine thirst for the Word.

Now that I am older, my sympathies have swung toward Martha. Maybe the reason is that I, too, know what it is like to be distracted with much serving. I, too, know what it is like to stand in the door of a hot kitchen, mopping my face with a dish towel, struggling against simmering resentments. (My sister will undoubtedly enjoy that admission!)

Yet I wonder whether it is a mistake to see this as a story about sibling rivalry. Perhaps we are not meant to choose sides, to identify with *either* Mary *or* Martha. What if we were meant to see ourselves in both sisters—and to rec-ognize the gifts of both?

Mary's contributions are easier to identify. Jesus has her full attention. In Jesus' own words, she has "chosen the better part" (v. 42). Note, however, that his use of the comparative term "better" does not necessarily imply that Martha's part is bad—only that it is not so high a priority at that moment. Given the fact that the Messiah is seated in their living room, Mary's decision to drop everything seems pretty appropriate!

Notice, too, his addition of the words "which will not be taken away from her." This phrase has always made me think that Jesus had spent a few hours in the kitchen him-self. They are the words of someone who knows what it feels like to spend hours preparing a meal, only to have it disappear "in the twinkling of an eye." The fruit of Martha's labor will be gone in ten minutes; Mary's reward will be with her for the rest of her life.

There is no way around it: Jesus does commend Mary. Yet he does so in the gentlest of terms, subtly identifying with her sister's plight even as he praises Mary. And he prefaces the whole with "Martha, Martha," a double en-dearment that may be our first and best clue as to the tone of his moderate reproof.

What, then, of Martha's contributions to the story? Is there anything in her behavior we ought to emulate, es-pecially in a season that drives so many of us to distrac-tion?

Martha has gotten a lot of bad press over the years. What most of her critics fail to recognize is that it was Martha who invited Jesus in the first place. Verse 38 points this out quite plainly. When Jesus came to town, it says, "a woman named Martha welcomed him into her home." If Martha had not been so gracious, this famous (infamous?) episode would never have happened at all!

Hospitality is what Martha models for us. It is a gift that is held in the highest honor throughout the Bible. And it is an attitude of both home and heart that is highly appropriate during Advent. Jesus will not come, after all, if we do not invite him.

Yet Martha also unwittingly alerts us to the risks of such a welcome. It is easy to lose our focus in the midst of all the preparations. We are, like her, distracted with much serving. The key is never to lose sight of the fact that it is Jesus himself who is sitting in our living room. He may have many different faces, but it is the Word made flesh all the same. ("Just as you did it to one of the least of these who are members of my family, you did it to me," Matt. 25:40.)

Advent is a time when both Mary and Martha have a word from the Lord for us. "Listen!" Jesus says, "I am standing at the door knocking; if you hear my voice and open the door, I will come in to you and eat with you, and you with me" (Rev. 3:20). Come, Lord Jesus!

FOR REFLECTION:

1. Are you a Mary or a Martha? What could these two women learn from each other?

2. What would make our Christmas celebrations more hospitable to the guest of honor?

ELIJAH SEES AN ANALYST
1 Kings 19:1–18

hat would happen if the prophet Elijah paid a visit to an analyst?

A friend of mine once observed that you are not technically paranoid if someone really *is* out to get you. According to that line of logic, we cannot accuse the prophet Elijah of paranoia in 1 Kings 19. With the wicked queen Jezebel hot on his heels, it is clear that his fears are entirely justified.

As we read Elijah's story, however, there may be other psychoanalytic adjectives that spring to mind. Verse 4 finds him slumped under a solitary broom tree, praying to die. "Aha," mutters our imaginary analyst, "the patient is acutely depressed with suicidal tendencies."

Not that we can blame Elijah for these things. If Elijah had expected a reward for his courageous role in the contest on Mt. Carmel (chap. 18), he is apparently going to be disappointed. Instead of riding the wave of his success, he is fleeing for his life. And from the sounds of it, that life is nearly spent. His comment about being "no better than my ancestors" (v. 4), is his way of saying, "I'm as good as dead." The only reward he seeks now is for God to get it over with.

Glimpses of Glory

Fortunately for Elijah, God sees things differently. In a beautiful parable of the way grace sometimes sneaks up on us, an angel shows up with a picnic basket. Yet the angel has to wake Elijah and order him to eat. Elijah complies, but then promptly curls back up under his broom tree. The patient angel pokes him and urges him to eat again so that he will have strength for "the journey" (v. 7).

What journey? The only journey Elijah has in mind is a one-way trip to join his ancestors. Once again, however, God seems to see things differently. Elijah sets off in the strength of that miraculous meal and finds himself at Mt. Horeb.

The location alone should have given Elijah a glimmer that something significant was in the offing. (Horeb is another name for Sinai, the mountain where God appeared to Moses and gave him the Law.) When God questions Elijah about what he is doing there, however, Elijah sounds as discouraged as ever. After a few pointed reminders of his past acts of loyalty, he winds up with the refrain "I alone am left, and they are seeking my life to take it away."

Let's pause to peak over the shoulder of Elijah's analyst. Writing fills the page. Comments like "Patient seems resistant to help" occur at several points. The phrase "Is preoccupied with death and self" is underlined.

Just *how* preoccupied is obvious from what follows. God stages an elaborate visual aid, designed to demonstrate that God's presence is not always with the powerful. A rock-splitting wind, a deafening earthquake, and a raging fire all pass by. Yet God is not in any of them. Instead, God shows up in an unexpected guise: "a still, small voice," or even "the sound of a faint whisper."

The translation of this last phrase is essential for understanding God's point. It goes straight to the heart of Elijah's depression. Elijah may think that he is alone and that his voice is little more than a dying whisper. But according to the way God sees it, that is enough. God can speak through faint whispers too!

Elijah, of course, misses the point. His reply to God's repeated question, "What are you doing here?" is precisely what it was before. "I alone am left," he moans.

Perhaps God takes a peak over the analyst's shoulder at this point. God's prescription is for a healthy dose of behavior modification. Elijah is sent straight to work in verses 15–17. Yet in one final concession to Elijah's fragile state, God ends with a reminder that Elijah is not as alone as he thinks he is.

For all of our attention to Elijah, this passage really tells us more about God than the prophet. What a wonderful picture of God's patience! Over and over again, God attempts to break through Elijah's resistance and self-absorption. When all efforts fail, God still leaves Elijah with the assurance that he is not alone. More than anything else, this last act of grace should give those of us on the analyst's couch the courage to take up our bed and walk!

FOR REFLECTION:

1. Has God's grace ever snuck up on you?

2. What is the most encouraging part of this passage for you?

WHAT'S IN A NAME?

1 Samuel 25

ames, like hemlines, have their ups and downs. Matilda and Lester used to be big but seem to have stepped aside for Ashley and Drew. Ellen and Adam are staging an impressive comeback. There is even a mini-trend toward naming babies after continents. Visit several kindergarten classrooms and you could well encounter an Asia or an Africa.

And then there is Nabal, whose parents gave their child a name that means "fool." Could he have grown up to be anything other than the surly and shortsighted person described in 1 Samuel 25? His own wife advises us not to take him seriously, for "as his name is, so is he" (v. 25). To paraphrase her further, "Nabal is his name, and folly is his game."

Should we suspect Nabal's wife, Abigail, of an appalling lack of loyalty? We might, except that the events of this episode bear out her assessment. When David and his merry men come to call, Nabal sends them away with little more than insults. Not only is this a serious violation of the ancient law of hospitality, it also may be an instance of simple ingratitude. David and his men, though on the run themselves, have protected Nabal's shepherds from attack in the wilderness. David's description of this act of generosity (vv. 7–8) is confirmed by one of Nabal's servants. David's men, says the servant in glowing terms, "were very good to us . . . and were a wall to us both by night and by day" (vv. 15–16).

Abigail is everything her husband is not. (Is it mere coincidence that her name means "my father's joy"?) When she hears of Nabal's deadly faux pas, she whisks together the equivalent of twenty or thirty Thanksgiving dinners and rushes out to intercept David. (He and four hundred of his close personal friends are on their way to wipe out every male in Nabal's household.) Risking it all in one bold roll of the dice, she takes the blame on herself and pleads for David to overlook the folly of "this ill-natured fellow, Nabal" (v. 25).

Whatever we may think of David's tactics in this passage, he does have an eye for quality. He recognizes the wisdom in Abigail's words almost instantly. It probably doesn't hurt that she has come bearing gifts or that she is from a wealthy family he can well afford as an ally. But these things are in the story's periphery. At the center of its vision—and David's—are Abigail's words about the dangers of taking revenge (v. 26). She has kept him from making a mistake that could have jeopardized his relationship with God, and thus his future kingship (vv. 28–31). And with an astonishing rhetorical sleight of hand, she has done it while letting him think it was his own idea. At the end of her speech, Abigail asks David to remember her when he comes into his kingdom. Little does she know she will not have to wait that long.

Bible Portraits

After returning home to find her husband in a drunken stupor, Abigail elects to postpone the news of his close call until morning. Her announcement has a sobering effect. In fact, the narrator tells us that Nabal's "heart died within him" and "he became like a stone" (v. 37). In ten days' time he died, giving David a powerful example of God's being both willing and able to execute justice. As if to demonstrate that he has learned his lesson, David immediately woos wisdom for himself, and Abigail becomes his wife.

Foolishness and wisdom face off in this ancient story, and David is presented as having to choose between the two. Yet I find Abigail's choices every bit as instructive. In an age when marriages were arranged, she probably did not choose Nabal. (Such a choice would have been completely out of character!) But she did make some choices in the midst of her misery that one has to admire. Life rarely serves up simple situations. Her courage, selflessness, and quick thinking are an inspiration to all of us who seek to be faithful in trying circumstances. As her name is, so is she: her *heavenly* Father's joy.

FOR REFLECTION:

1. Where is wisdom in this story?

2. What are some of the most difficult choices you have had to make? What are some of the choices the church faces today? How do we find God's wisdom in the midst of these complex situations?

A LITTLE
GLIMPSE OF GLORY
John 20:1–18

ow is your peripheral vision? Most believers do not have any trouble seeing the pearl at the center of this passage, that is, the resurrection of Jesus Christ. But at the edge of the story is a lesser but lovely gem that we can only see from the corner of our interpretive eye. That gem is the friendship between Jesus and Mary Magdalene.

All we know about Mary from Magdala (a small town on the western shore of the Sea of Galilee) is what we can piece together from the gospels. Luke tells us that she had once been possessed by seven demons, but that Jesus had driven them out (Luke 8:2). From that time forward, she seems to have been among Jesus' staunchest supporters, providing for him from her own personal means (Luke 8:3). Her devotion extended even to the cross and the tomb; all four gospel writers attest to her presence at both. Because she brought the news of the empty tomb to the disciples, Augustine called her "the apostle to the apostles."

John's version of the Easter story has Mary Magdalene showing up at the graveyard "while it was still dark." This was a doubly dangerous thing for Mary to do. First, she would have been vulnerable to attack at that time of day.

Second, there were strict laws forbidding public mourning for executed criminals. According to at least one early source, those who mourned for someone who had been crucified risked the same fate themselves.

Why take the risk? John gives us no specifics, but in view of Mary's demeanor throughout the rest of the story, it makes sense to assume that it is a measure of her love for Jesus. She is clearly past caring for her own safety. Note, for instance, her lack of reaction to the angels in verse 12. This is one of the few instances in scripture where the presence of an angel does not provoke abject terror. Usually, angels must preface their announcements with an obligatory, "Fear not," but here they simply ask, "Woman, why are you weeping?" (v. 13).

Mary's answer indicates that she does not realize the implications of the empty tomb. "They have taken away my Lord, and I do not know where they have laid him," she sobs. No wonder she's upset. Just when she thinks things cannot possibly get worse, they do. Someone has apparently robbed her of even the rituals of grief.

Mary's despair is so deep that she does not recognize Jesus when she turns and sees him. It is only when she hears her name on his lips that the incredible truth hits home. He is alive! "Rabbouni!" she gasps, a word that means "My teacher," or perhaps even "My dear teacher." Then she does what anyone would do under such incredible circumstances: she embraces him. We can only infer this last part, of course, on the basis of Jesus' words in verse 17, "Do not hold on to me. . . ." But we ought not conclude that Jesus' objection arose from any aversion for Mary. In fact, his explanation affirms their relationship in the closest possible terms. As he entrusts her with the news of his resurrection and ascension, he claims her as his sister in the newborn faith ("my Father and your Father . . . "). He is, of course, still her "Lord," as well (v. 18), but who can read his last words to her without hearing the affection and joy with which they must have been spoken?

Modern moviemakers have had a field day with this relationship, insisting that Jesus and Mary were lovers. In a culture where all roads seem to lead to sex, their approach is hardly surprising. Yet it is precisely because our culture is so obsessed with sex that this passage—and the memory of Jesus' and Mary Magdalene's relationship—is so important.

Jesus' divinity does not detract from this passage's portrait of a beautiful friendship between a man and a woman. Sex is clearly out of the question. But shared sorrow, deep joy, and a common sense of calling are not. It may not be the central point of this passage, but if we look out of the corner of our eye, we can catch a little glimpse of glory here. That glimpse reminds us of how very beautiful it is to be "brother and sister" in Christ.

NOTES

1. I am indebted to my friend and former student Joshua Blunt for pointing me to the parallels between this passage and Genesis 29.

2. John Milton, *Paradise Lost* (New York, Scarborough, Ontario: Mentor Books, 1961;1981), Book IX, Line 999.

3. Edwin Muir, *Collected Poems* (New York: Oxford University Press, 1960), 227.

4. C. S. Lewis, *Mere Christianity* (New York: MacMillan Publishing Co., 1952), 33.

5. Frederick Buechner, *Whistling in the Dark* (San Francisco: HarperSanFrancisco, 1988), 29.

6. Robert Southwell, *Complete Poems* (Westport, Connecticut: Greenwood Press, 1970), 111–112.

7. Emily Dickinson, *The Complete Poems of Emily Dickinson*, ed. Thomas H. Johnson (Boston: Little, Brown and Company, 1960), 160.

8. I am indebted to friends and former students Aimee Wallis Buchanan and Bill Buchanan for this important insight.

9. William Holladay, *The Psalms through Three Thousand Years* (Minneapolis: Fortress Press, 1993), 11–12.

10. From a sermon by Karen Pidcock-Lester, Second Presbyterian Church, Richmond, Virginia, October, 1992.

11. Lewis B. Smedes, *How Can It Be All Right When Everything Is All Wrong* (San Francisco: Harper & Row, 1982), 17.

12. I am indebted to my friend and colleague Timothy Brown for this story.

13. George Eliot, *Adam Bede* (New York: Penguin Books, 1980), 168.

14. George Eliot, *Romola* (London: Oxford University Press, 1965), 372.

15. John Calvin, *Genesis* (Grand Rapids: Baker Book House, 1979), 568.

16. George Eliot, *Middlemarch* (New York: Penguin Books, 1985), 226.

17. C. S. Lewis, *A Grief Observed* (New York: Seabury Press, 1963), 32, 35.

18. *Ibid.*, 37.